belair
LEADERS

ART AND DESIGN
Primary Coordinator's Handbook

By John Bowden
with Susan Ogier and Peter Gregory

Dedication

This book is a tribute to the career of John Bowden and is dedicated to his grandchildren, Mia and Josef.

Published by Collins
An imprint of HarperCollins*Publishers*
The News Building
1 London Bridge Street
London
SE1 9GF

© HarperCollins*Publishers* Limited 2013

10 9 8 7 6 5 4

ISBN 978-0-00-745563-8

British Library Cataloguing in Publication Data
A Catalogue record for this publication is available from the British Library

Internal and cover design by Steve Evans Design and Illustration
Written by John Bowden, Susan Ogier and Peter Gregory
Project managed by Dawn Booth
Edited by Jane Moses
Proofread by Fiona Undrill
Index by Michael Forder
Photographs: pp. 6, 8, 10, 11, 16, 17 top, 19, 20, 25, 41, 43, 46, 47, 48, 49, 50, 52, 53, 54, 55, 56, 61, 62, 65, 69, 70 Nigel Meager; pp. 7, 9, 15, 17 bottom, 21, 22, 26, 34, 37, 44, 57, 60, 63, 66, 67, 68 Elmcroft Studios; pp. 13, 23, 28, 29, 31, 35, 36, 42, 58 bottom, 59. 64, 80 Arted EU Limited and Elmcroft Studios; pp. 18, 33, 38, 40 taken at The Robert and Lisa Sainsbury Collection, the University of East Anglia by Nigel Meager in 2011; pp. 39, 58 top © Brandon Bourdages/shutterstock.com; p. 51 © Susan Ogier

Browse the complete Collins catalogue at
www.collins.co.uk

Contents

Introduction

I am very privileged to introduce the Belair Leaders *Art and Design Primary Coordinator's Handbook*, a new edition of the *Primary Art and Design Subject Leaders' Handbook*, initially researched and written by John Bowden (Collins Educational, 2006).

John Bowden was a man of great ability, talent, energy, charm and charisma, dedicated to improving Art and Design education across all phases of education. His dedication served us well; many hundreds of teachers in both the primary and secondary phases have been inspired by his teaching both in Initial Teacher Education and within the context of professional development as they moved through their teaching careers.

As senior Art and Design advisor for North Yorkshire for 26 years, John had first-hand experience of primary classroom practice and the vital need for continuing professional development (CPD) for primary teachers of Art and Design as they moved towards subject leadership. His work with Initial Teacher Education gave him particular insight and understanding of adult learning within the context of subject knowledge and pedagogy.

John's engagement in his subject was immersive and contagious. He was also a practising artist; John painted and drew, in what he described as a 'modernist' style, vigorous paintings that explored colour, shape and form from a starting point of a place or something 'seen'. John also had the hands-on ability to make, to create, and to fashion structures out of cardboard and clay and wood that could be achieved in the classroom with modest resources and big ambitions.

Before his untimely death in January 2012, John had begun to revise and update the *Handbook* for Collins Learning in partnership with the National Society for Education in Art and Design (NSEAD). Typically, John had brought massive enthusiasm and many new ideas to the project and it needed both expertise, sensitivity and commitment to continue.

At that point, primary Art and Design experts Susan Ogier from the University of Roehampton and Peter Gregory from Canterbury Christ Church University stepped forward to complete the revision. They realised that not only is the *Handbook* very much needed, but also that it is a celebration and tribute to John Bowden's lifetime commitment to Art and Design education.

I was lucky enough to observe first hand John Bowden sharing his vast experience, when we took the *Handbook* on the road for a national programme of NSEAD one-day courses for emerging primary Art and Design coordinators. I watched teachers at the beginning of the day, nervous of the subject, unsure of what area within the subject to tackle next, and John did not diminish either the complexities or the challenges of the subject. Art and Design was not to be reassuring and easy, and leadership is always going to be a challenge. Yet by the end of the day the teachers were empowered, confident and ready to go back into the classroom, not just with new-found skills but also with sustainable strategies that were going to make an immediate difference.

His advocacy gave many primary teachers of Art and Design the inspiration and ideas to work with renewed creativity and confidence, back in the classroom.

This is why the book is so important: it captures that spirit and energy and the unique power and value of Art and Design in education. It shows not how to teach the subject, but why, what its value is and its importance.

The Belair Leaders *Art and Design Primary Coordinator's Handbook* will give teachers who want to lead their schools in Art and Design, the courage and confidence to put the subject at the heart of the curriculum, and show that it can play an important part in every subject in the primary classroom.

Lesley Butterworth

General Secretary

NSEAD

Part 1: Planning for Art and Design

Leading Art and Design

Every primary school should appoint a subject coordinator responsible for leading Art and Design. Whether you are an Art and Design specialist or an interested novice this is an important, exciting and rewarding role. You will have the opportunity to influence a visually stimulating environment throughout the whole school, which fosters a vitality and love of learning: an essential part of life in any primary school. By encouraging the teachers in your school to develop their own abilities in teaching Art and Design you will all be able to pass on important skills to the children in your care.

What the role means

The Ofsted report on Art and Design, *Making a Mark: Art, Craft and Design Education 2008–2011* (2012), highlights the value of the role of Art and Design coordinator (also known as Art and Design leader), pointing out that '…high standards are found where there is strong subject leadership underpinned by a commitment to the subject from the head teacher'.

Some primary schools are fortunate enough to have a dedicated teacher for Art and Design who works throughout the school, either visiting individual classes or working from a specialist Art room. In most cases, however, generalist primary teachers are responsible for all curriculum subjects. It is therefore vital for someone in the school to take responsibility for developing all teachers' awareness in Art and Design.

Subject coordinators usually specialise in one subject area, but often they have a large portfolio of responsibilities, especially if the school is small. Some will have great enthusiasm and willingness to take on Art and Design, but lack an Art and Design-trained background and lack confidence in their expertise. In addition, available time for subject leadership is often very limited and, understandably, some Art and Design coordinators admit that professional development is cut short by the demands of everyday teaching.

Therefore, while this role is important and exciting, it is also particularly challenging. It cannot be fulfilled effectively without commitment.

Accepting the role

Ideally, as subject coordinator you will have had some training in Art and Design, although you may well not be a 'specialist'. However it is possible that you have inherited the position despite your limited background. Some head teachers specifically choose to rotate subject coordinator roles and responsibilities; however, while this does offer additional career experience, it can be counterproductive. If teachers are regularly given new roles, then there will inevitably be limitations on their expertise and personal interests.

A further challenge is that not all initial teacher education courses offer an Art and Design component, or give much time to such activities if they do. It is often no more than an introduction, due to time constraints and government priorities. You may not have had specialist training for teaching Art and Design, and neither might the other teachers in your school.

Developing subject expertise

Whatever your experience, the first thing is to undertake a personal audit of your own knowledge and understanding (see Chapter 3: How is your school doing? and Appendix 2: Subject coordinator's staff questionnaire). Knowing what you do not know is the first stage of your development and this is just part of being a reflective teacher. Indeed, further and regular continuing professional development (CPD) is essential if, as subject coordinator, you are to build and maintain good subject knowledge and develop your skill and expertise.

Choosing CPD

The National Society for Education in Art and Design (NSEAD) (www.nsead.org) is a suitable first stop when you are looking for examples of good practice and CPD events. There are also other ways you can go about increasing your knowledge and skills, and, on one hand, this could be as simple as visiting local galleries and exhibitions. You might, on the other hand, bring an expert in to school to provide training for the whole staff, or you could share this type of workshop within a 'cluster' of local subject coordinators, as this will enable you to share costs.

It is important to select CPD according to your particular needs.

If you have a limited Art background, or want skills refreshment, you might need some practical 'hands-on' activity to learn about basic materials and processes. If, however, you have a secure understanding of the subject, then a specialist course or one exploring the subject coordinator's role in greater depth may be more appropriate. Reading widely on the subject and using relevant websites and journals will also be useful in developing your wider knowledge.

The world of Art and Design education is constantly changing and as the person charged with coordinating the subject in your school you must try to keep abreast of new developments.

Recognising good practice

Even if you are fairly confident in your own abilities in Art and Design, a personal audit will reveal that there is still much more for you to learn. You can interpret this as a very positive outcome, and you should now begin to feel excited about your own new learning in the task ahead. The job of becoming a strong subject coordinator in Art and Design is all about self-reflection and questioning your own practice as well as that of your colleagues. It is about recognising what outstanding Art and Design teaching is like, and this is explored throughout this book.

2 What is an Art and Design coordinator?

Many of the roles and responsibilities of the subject coordinator apply across the board to every subject in the National Curriculum (NC). However, each subject area has different challenges, and demands specific knowledge, skills and understanding. A practical subject such as Art and Design presents special consideration of the organisation and management of artistic media, as well as developing the confidence of the staff team. This chapter will outline the ways in which you, as the proactive Art and Design coordinator, can explore ways of raising the profile of the subject within the school to ensure that it is taught effectively and given independence and status.

Why have coordinators?

Inevitably, in many primary schools, priority and status may be given to Literacy and Numeracy, as these are key indicators when evaluating the performance of the school itself and individual pupils against national criteria. In addition, over recent years Ofsted inspectors have been very concerned that Art and Design has been seen either as a vehicle for 'servicing other subjects' or sacrificed in the mistaken belief that this will somehow raise standards elsewhere in the curriculum.

This may be a challenge in the current educational climate, however many primary schools recognise the unique contribution that Art and Design can make to the development of primary pupils. It is in these schools that enthusiastic subject coordinators can be found driving developments forward with interest and determination.

Development planning

The Art and Design coordinator should start their development planning with an audit of the current practice in the school, identifying subject strengths and areas for development, as well as recognising the limitations relating to teacher expertise and resources.

An audit of your staff's skill and understanding will be an invaluable activity at this point (see Appendix 2: Subject coordinator's staff questionnaire).

Ideally, everyone teaching in the school should be involved in this Art and Design audit.

Once the responses are analysed, you should be able to identify a number of clearly indicated development areas that can be prioritised in order. Development needs will vary according to the school context – and do remember that not everything can be done at once. The final outcome of this process should be a development plan that is the focus for change. This will provide a development 'diary' to inform others staff of the way to proceed in the teaching of Art and Design, this could include the head teacher, governors or even an outside agency such as Ofsted. A framework for analysing your current situation and planning for development is presented in Chapter 3: How is your school doing? Many schools require subject coordinators to create and update a file of information based on their development plan.

Establishing your policy and a scheme of work

Establishing the policy and scheme of work is a key responsibility for the Art and Design coordinator and should reflect the ethos and organisation of Art and Design across the school. Without such documentation there cannot be a coherent and consistent whole-school approach to the subject. The Art and Design curriculum should be broad, balanced and address any statutory requirements, and your documentation should identify how far your ambitions for the subject have been shared with staff. There should be clear evidence of agreement about the ways that Art and Design will be taught across the school.

There are three related parts to a typical set of school subject documents:

- A policy which is a general statement of intent related to key aspects of the delivery of the subject, presenting aims and objectives, assessment strategies, strategies for differentiation according to ability, principles for inclusion and so on. It is important that this is school specific, and you should avoid commercially available policies.
- The curriculum plan (scheme of work) which outlines the programme of skills, knowledge and understanding that will be taught to each year group consistently to ensure progression across the school.
- The third section that many subject coordinators provide to encourage staff to raise standards, is a guidance document – in the form of an appendix – which offers help to anyone wishing to extend his or her teaching skills or appreciate fully the properties of differing media.

The Art and Design subject coordinator will need to understand the essential contents of a policy, and the procedures that are necessary to establish an effective and usable scheme of work. If the school has no current scheme of work, it may be helpful to use a template for planning a sample overall plan, which can be modified according to school needs.

As important is that the rest of the staff want to adopt the principles and content of these documents, and they need to be actively involved in their development through a series of staff training activities.

Identifying staff development

You may have identified from staff responses to the audit that some staff need assistance and guidance. Each member of staff has a right to appropriate training, however in primary schools it is unlikely to be possible for individuals to receive external subject training due to cost and time constraints. Therefore the subject coordinator will need to arrange and deliver 'in house' in-service training, having identified particular needs; these could be to develop specific skills which might have been identified as lacking through the audit process. For example you might find that teachers are unfamiliar with techniques, such as sculpting, using wire and plaster bandage, or clay, etc.

Small schools can often get together to share their common expertise and training activities.

Establishing an assessment policy

Generally, assessment in Art and Design in the primary school has been underdeveloped, despite the introduction some years ago in England of NC levels for assessment purposes at the end of each key stage. This is partly because these levels were complex. A further constraint on assessment procedures is the common belief that Art and Design 'cannot be assessed', confusing the absolute judgements made in information-centred subjects, such as Mathematics, with the criterion-based and moderated procedures used by creative subjects.

The Art and Design subject coordinator needs to devise and defend a manageable assessment system. This should be understood by all staff and used consistently throughout the school so that pupils know what they have to do in order to improve and progress. A portfolio of exemplar materials, containing examples of a range of pupils' work, can be assembled and collected according to year groups. Standards of achievement, which could be measured against learning intentions and specified criteria, could be established and reviewed regularly as a staff development activity.

You are ultimately responsible for ensuring that effective assessment procedures have been established for the subject and that systematic assessment takes place.

Monitoring teaching and learning

It is important to monitor the quality of teaching in Art and Design and the delivery of the subject throughout the school, both in terms of the curriculum coverage and standards achieved. Opportunities for doing this may be limited and will require the understanding and support of senior subject coordinators in the school – especially as resources will be needed to complete the tasks.

Ofsted has commented that the one area where practice continues to remain underdeveloped – despite its importance – is the monitoring of teaching in Art and Design. To be effective, monitoring the subject must involve lesson observation and this should be done in a non-threatening manner by agreeing an observation schedule with teachers in advance. This can easily be achieved by adapting or extending the existing observation schedules that are currently used.

In addition, the subject coordinator should take any opportunity to look at pupils' work produced in lessons or displayed in classrooms. Medium-term planning for Art and Design should also be collected regularly from every class or year group by the subject coordinator. In this way, they can ensure that the subject is taught consistently, as well as recorded and assessed effectively. Much can be learned by informal monitoring procedures although, ideally, active classroom observation and support should be also taking place.

The important thing, particularly in larger schools, is to gain an overview of what is happening in all classrooms to give you a clear picture so that you can address any potential weaknesses.

Managing resources

There should be a budget for the subject's consumable items, although this is likely to be limited. A wise subject coordinator will be able to tap into other budgets for more expensive items or equipment that will enhance pupils' Art experiences in school. Each year, the subject coordinator will have the responsibility for either spending this budget and/or advising other staff on the most appropriate materials and equipment to purchase.

Significant resource expenditure should be driven by long-term needs identified in the development plan, rather than individual short-term staff demands.

Systems for delivery and distribution of these resources are also the responsibility of the Art and Design coordinator and it is important to ensure that these are consistent, seen to be fair and avoid wasting resources. Some resources will be kept centrally and shared (for example, resources such as posters or specialist equipment), while others will be held in individual classrooms (for example, basic Art and Design materials). In some schools, the day-to-day management of materials may be delegated to a trained teaching assistant.

An innovative curriculum

Effective leadership and coordination of the subject involves innovation (sometimes with open-ended outcomes) as well as organisation. Exciting art- and design work may be produced by using 'artists and designers in schools' effectively, or in 'Art and Design weeks' when the regular curriculum is suspended, allowing concentration for a longer period on one subject. Such initiatives are usually the result of imaginative thinking by the subject coordinator.

Managing transition

Pupil portfolios of art- and design work produced across the key stages ensure that the subject coordinator is in a very influential position to make the transition between classes clear, informative and developmental.

This is also the case for transition between Key Stages 2 and 3 (ages 11–12). What you do need to avoid is for your pupils to be given tasks in secondary school that repeat what they have already done at primary level. If your school feeds into a local secondary school you might arrange a visit to the Art and Design department to establish contact and share practice.

Secondary teachers should be cooperative if you take this initiative, as once they are confident that pupils who transfer at the end of Key Stage 2 (ages 7–11) have a consistent understanding of the subject and possess common basic skills, there will be no reason for them to treat every Year 7 (ages 11–12) pupil as a complete beginner or novice.

Subject-coordinator support

It is also important to establish support for your own development, and it is useful if local subject coordinators for Art and Design meet as a 'cluster' or other network group. If you're not sure how to find these, your head teacher should be able to help. NSEAD has encouraged the development of regional groups, so contact them for advice. You will find confidence and encouragement from others in a similar position as well as hearing about the opportunities for sharing local projects, resources or news of forthcoming Art and Design exhibitions.

Leading Art and Design is a challenging role and the list of responsibilities may seem daunting, but it does, of course, represent the ideal, which may not be deliverable in every school. Different contexts provide different constraints, but they also produce new and exciting opportunities. What is clear is that without your active and confident leadership, the subject is unlikely to flourish.

3 How is your school doing?

You might now be feeling slightly overwhelmed by the range of activities you need to undertake as part of your role as subject coordinator. After you have completed your audit you should establish a development plan. As a proactive subject coordinator for Art and Design you will want to move practice forward by making changes that have been agreed, and are supported by staff. Any weaknesses identified in previous inspections should also be taken into account. The development plan states your ambition for change and everyone should know what you want them to focus on to achieve the goals.

The development plan

Your development plan has to prioritise issues, as there are likely to be more areas for development than can be achieved over a three-year planning cycle (although some schools use a five-year period). Usually, development plans are presented as a table, with columns for each stated development objective.

These objectives should explain:

- why that area has been identified for development activity
- the strategy that will achieve it
- who will be responsible for monitoring progress
- what resource implications there are (if any)
- when the objective will be achieved
- how its success will be measured.

Table 1. Example of a development plan

Art and Design	Strategic plan	2014–2015			Three-dimensional work
Context	Strategic action(s)	Lead	Resources	Completion date	Measurement of success
Scrutiny of teachers' plans showed underdevelopment of three-dimensional activities (2013–2014)	Coordinator to support staff	Sarah	Planned leadership time	Across year: end June 2015	Improved confidence level (staff audit July 2015)
Staff audit revealed lack of knowledge, skills and confidence with particular materials (July 2014)	INSET activity	Sarah/Rachel	Two staff meetings devoted to three-dimensional practical sessions (autumn/spring) Additional materials (£40 agreed)	By end December 2014 (meeting 1) By end April 2015 (meeting 2)	Evaluations following meetings
	Creative practitioner to develop project alongside class teachers, leading to exhibition	Sarah/HT	Discuss project with Cluster (regular meeting)	Cluster meeting due February 2015	Project successfully funded and implemented Cluster presentation (and report to staff and governors)
	Shared adult/pupil three-dimensional exhibition (open to parents and governors)	Rachel	Submit bid by end Spring Term (£350?) Additional planning time (Sarah/Rachel)	Bid submitted by 30 March 2015 End April 2015 (HT to confirm when budget agreed)	Bid submitted and funds obtained April 2015 Planning time included in 2015 staff activity plan
Next planned audits by Sarah: **Plans: January 2015** **Staff audit: July 2015**		Sarah	Resources for exhibition (£50?) from PTA Opportunities to produce/ sell programmes at exhibition	PTA meeting planned early April 2015 Exhibition probably June 2015 prior to Open Day	Successful exhibition held summer 2015

Prioritising objectives

The audit is essentially for your personal use as subject coordinator, however your development objectives are difficult to devise without consulting others. To decide independently and arbitrarily what is going to be targeted in a development plan will achieve little, as development objectives cannot be attained without whole-staff support. Therefore, if all staff are to have ownership of the development process, the strategy used to identify and prioritise objectives needs to be transparent. Every member of staff needs to be involved and consulted. You could be even more radical and also ask some pupils and their parents what they would like to change in their Art and Design education.

Simply asking staff in a staff meeting what changes they feel are necessary will not be constructive. Some staff may have particular and idiosyncratic views and others may be just indifferent or ignorant about the subject as a whole. Your strategy should be two-fold. First, systematically assess what is (and, just as importantly, what is not) taking place by making your own observations of current practice within the school and completing the subject coordinator's checklist that is Appendix 1.

You will see that the survey comprises a series of questions, each of which requires a 'Yes / No' response. It may be that you cannot make such absolute judgements, although the 'Yes – But' case will mean that you are starting to delve deeper into the particular situation at your school. As a starting point this checklist can be enlightening because, in theory, any question that you have given a negative response to is a potential area for development and your process of analysis will have begun.

Second, consult staff using a formal questionnaire, such as in Appendix 2, to reinforce your informal information-gathering. Remember that your survey is based on each person's particular viewpoint about best practice in primary Art and Design education. Not everyone will agree, especially if there has been little basic pedagogical thinking about Art and Design among the staff. Even if you disagree with the perspective of a certain viewpoint, the document will serve an important purpose in helping you to define your own, personal philosophy.

Look at your responses carefully; there may be, from your perspective, very clear and valid reasons for the answers given. For instance, although there should be a balanced programme of two-dimensional and three-dimensional work, your school might have acknowledged this but has nevertheless consciously prioritised one particular area. This may be to capitalise on staff strengths or ensure adequate depth of experience for pupils at this time (see Chapter 5: Planning for Art and Design). If this is the case, you will obviously choose not to select it as a development area. Equally, you may have already considered and rejected an identified development area highlighted by the honest completion of this checklist because of significant and insurmountable constraints; for instance you might recognise the need for children to experience making large-scale work, but classroom space could make this ambition unrealistic for the time being. In this way, by using the checklist analytically and flexibly as a basis for group discussion, your individual school Art and Design development priorities can be established.

Remember that reaching a decision about whether to prioritise a development area must draw on all the information you have gathered, as well as upon your audit. Look at work on classroom walls and in folders, talk with staff and pupils who are eager to show you their work, and see how effectively materials are both organised and presented. Formal lesson observation will provide even more evidence.

All this information should be taken into account before decisions are made. Your final development plan must be realistic, and be achievable in the timescale identified. In addition, the staff questionnaire will provide a different perspective. The staff questionnaire is shown as Appendix 2.

Developing your vision

The ultimate test of your effectiveness as a subject coordinator is the extent to which you are able to influence practice in Art and Design education and institute lasting change throughout the school. The aim is to ensure a consistent and positive experience for every pupil, and this can be quite a challenge. The subject coordinator should lead by example: as a shining beacon of personal good practice. However the sad truth is that some staff may neither recognise your efforts, nor be easily influenced by them.

Putting your plans into practice

Some new subject coordinators find they have inherited their role in a school where everything needs to change. By completing the checklist in Appendix 1, towards the end of the book, you might have already identified examples of poor practice in Art and Design teaching, including a lack of expertise and confidence among the staff or inconsistency in how school policy is implemented in this subject. Some staff might even show indifference and a resistance to change. These factors, among others, can lead to low standards in teaching and in children's attainment and enjoyment of Art and Design, but it is possible for you to make a marked difference if your subject leadership is tactful and purposeful.

You must initially get as many people on your side as possible and you would do well to begin with the senior managers in your school. The starting place is to make an appointment with your head teacher, in which you can discuss ideas for your development plan. These ideas should arise naturally from the previously conducted audit.

Primary head teachers are, in general, committed to providing a broad and balanced curriculum for the children in their schools; however they are subject to external pressures of the national agenda. The school's position in league tables and children's Literacy and Numeracy scores may inevitably be a priority.

This can lead to subjects such as Art and Design becoming side-lined and being given low status in school improvement planning. Your personal drive and passion for the subject will help here, and if you can convince the head teacher of your vision for change, then the rest of the senior management team will follow.

Trying to change everything at once is unrealistic and will only gain you the reputation of being an Art and Design extremist, which is not the best position from which to exert influence. The wise subject coordinator will have sensible and strategic ambitions, recognising that their powers for action may be limited in the short term but their capacity to influence is unbounded.

A tactfully presented long-term strategy which shows clear priorities is much more likely to achieve the permanent change that increases the impact of Art and Design in the school. Your plan will not be without costs, so you should prepare a request for a specific budget for Art and Design to carry it out.

Sharing your vision

As subject coordinator you can begin to capitalise on all opportunities to talk about Art and Design and share the contents of your development plan. These might be in formal circumstances such as while leading a staff meeting, or informally by helping colleagues link topic work through Art and Design. Every opportunity should be taken to show your enthusiasm and willingness to help other staff. You can also assist by speaking plainly and avoiding the use of specialist terms and jargon.

Try always to be readily available and willing to give advice, referring staff to the part of your scheme of work which offers guidance on planning, materials and processes (how to produce this is discussed in Chapter 5: Planning for Art and Design). Part 2 of this book can also be used for this purpose.

Create a folder of web resources showing techniques, materials and ideas for activities linked to learning, and place it on the school computer's shared drive. It should contain articles on processes or themes, alongside gallery sites and artists' and designers' images, which will supplement the main resources.

Consulting staff

Once you have the senior managers listening to your ideas, it is time to recruit the rest of the staff. To do this, you will need to have established your policy, a clear scheme of work and implemented manageable assessment procedures. It is essential to involve all staff and, wherever possible, use their ideas and favourite artists, although not at the expense of abandoning the key principles that underpin good practice. Imposing a policy without consultation will ensure that some members of staff will surreptitiously subvert it, or even simply ignore it.

Your audit is the tool that will identify all key issues for Art and Design, but it is not intended for use with the whole staff. It is, however, equally important to research what everybody else in the school thinks about the subject, so that you gain a realistic picture of individual teacher's attitudes and their current knowledge and abilities in Art and Design. It will also act as a curriculum development document, as it touches on many of the aspects of best practice.

You might consider using the Subject coordinator's staff questionnaire provided as Appendix 2 towards the end of this book, which is more straightforward and aimed specifically for the generalist teacher. This will give you a clear picture for ascertaining priorities for training. The questionnaire is a way for teachers to communicate with the subject coordinator in a personal way or even, if they wish, anonymously. Individual reflection and open-ended responses are invited.

Feedback

The answers you receive may be unexpected and sometimes rather negative, but the questionnaire will also identify teachers who are positive about Art and Design, even if they lack the expertise to move the subject forward. These are your allies who will be important supporters in subject initiatives in the future: a group of enthusiasts can achieve much more than any one individual.

The responses to the questionnaire may show that some teachers are not devoting a specific period of time to focused Art and Design teaching or, at worst, are merely using the subject as an opportunity to occupy and entertain children. Try to see these attitudes as starting points for change rather than a barrier to development.

Providing support

The staff questionnaire deals with the delicate issue of direct observation of classes by the subject coordinator. This is because teachers most in need of help in a practical subject such as Art and Design are probably the ones who are most likely to be intimidated by the process of direct observation. Giving colleagues the option of having the subject coordinator work alongside them, or even teaching their class while they watch, is more tactful than simply telling them that you will observe formally and then offering a list of ways on how their lesson could have been improved. Tactfulness and encouragement are the watchwords here.

Drawing together

You might, try to give Art and Design a specific focus for learning. Why not suggest an 'Art and Design afternoon' once a month, or an 'Art and Design week' once a year, where activities concentrate on an aspect of the subject related to a particular or common theme across the whole school?

Your opportunity to influence what goes on will increase if colleagues, identified from the questionnaire as friends of the subject, are involved in planning and delivering the events. Why not contact a local college to ask if some teacher trainees could be involved, or even sixth formers studying Art and Design from a local secondary school? Their enthusiasm will be a catalyst for success.

Providing training

Part of your role will be to provide training for members of staff. It may be that staff responses reveal needs that are different from the ones you identified through the original audit. Sometimes inexperienced staff are looking for CPD in Art and Design that provides 'quick tips' for lesson activities, rather than in-depth examination of Art and Design education issues. However CPD must accommodate everyone's perceived needs if it is to have any useful impact. When it is the turn of Art and Design for a staff training session, try initially to make the experience memorable, entertaining and non-threatening. Practical activities are most successful if they are collaborative exercises and involve problem-solving with materials, particularly in three-dimensional, or processes that can be demonstrated and then tried out in pairs or small groups. Successful CPD activities mean everyone leaves the group with a sense of satisfaction and a positive desire for more, rather than exposing individual inadequacies. Further suggestions for staff development activities are provided at the end of many of the chapters in Part 2.

Reflection

A final recommendation to you as Art and Design coordinator, once you have gathered in all the feedback, is to take the long-term view of development. There may well be those who, whatever your best efforts, continue to look at Art and Design education with scepticism. This is inevitable and you should not be discouraged. As more staff adopt the practices you advocate, the more likely it is that the resistant minority will also begin to take notice and the quality of all pupils' creative experiences will be further improved. The future of Art and Design education in primary schools is in your hands.

5 | Planning for Art and Design

You now have a picture of the practice and views of staff and this will have informed your development plan. As a result of what you have learned it is likely that you will need to review your paperwork. After all, while most primary schools can produce a basic Art and Design policy, some still lack an effective scheme of work, detailing the paths of progression expected to be offered by pupils. The documentation may not have been designed specifically for your particular school; it may have been developed as a result of comments by an inspector or an adviser, in response to new national initiatives, or simply as part of a regular cycle of curriculum development.

So, while your school almost certainly has some Art and Design documentation, it is quite possible that it needs revision and updating This chapter considers the dilemmas facing you as a subject coordinator who needs to produce documentation that will underpin the process of change. It also outlines key requirements, so that you can compare what is currently in place in your school with an ideal situation.

Key documents

Art and Design documentation is considered in three categories:

1. The first is the policy statement, which can be divided into sections giving brief statements on aims, assessment, equal opportunities and so on.

2. The second is the scheme of work (also called a curriculum plan) which outlines what will be taught to pupils.

3. The third section comprises further guidance and is effectively a staff Art and Design handbook.

For more details on these, see Chapter 2: What is an Art and Design coordinator?

Linking assessment processes to the above documentation is covered in more detail in Chapter 6: Recording progress.

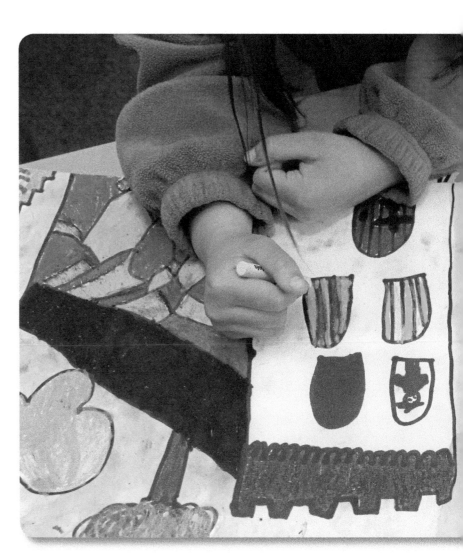

The policy statement

The Art and Design policy statement is the easier part. By following the outline below you will probably gain a picture of practice in your school, although it must be tailored according to individual or local needs. A policy is fairly simple to write but, as we all know, it can be more difficult to implement. It is essential that it should reflect a balance between a vision for improvement in the subject and the reality of the school's Art and Design practice, rather than present an idealised picture. Someone will eventually measure policy statements against actual practice, so rhetorical statements should always be avoided.

Each policy statement in the policy document should be brief; if it is necessary to provide detailed information about procedures and practice, this should be provided in an appendix. Neither should Art and Design policy merely repeat generic statements that are available in other general school policy documents; it should focus specifically on Art and Design.

What to include

The policy should include brief statements on:

- The rationale – the mission statement that underpins the school's philosophy for the subject, and may be derived from a key document on Art and Design education or quote a key point from a leading Art and Design educator explaining the importance of the subject in the primary school.
- The aims and objectives – these can vary depending on the school but are likely to include: development of visual awareness and visual literacy in pupils; using Art and Design to record inner feelings and express creative imagination; development of pupils' understanding of the visual elements of Art and Design; development of pupils' critical thinking; understanding pupils' own and others' cultural heritage; using artistic media to acquire skills and develop techniques.
- Organisation and management of the subject – should be outlined briefly. Will Art and Design be taught only through topic work? If so, ensure that high-quality separate subject teaching occurs. Alternatively, perhaps Art and Design will be organised into blocks of time throughout each year.

- Teaching style – it is now recognised that a wide range of teaching styles, involving whole-class demonstration, time for discussion and reflection, individual as well as group work, are necessary if effective, focused Art and Design teaching is to take place. These should foster pupil experimentation and not limit the outcomes.
- Your role as subject coordinator – although this should already be available in other whole-school documentation; this might be a generic statement covering the responsibilities of all subject coordinators.
- It might also include a policy on differentiation for Art and Design, which is likely to be achieved largely by teacher observations and individual outcomes. Make it clear that specific, differentiated tasks should target individual children at all levels of ability.
- Policy on equal opportunities – key points are to avoid stereotyping in relation to the gender/ethnic background of any artists or designers being studied, and make a positive effort to celebrate cultural diversity. All pupils should feel able to participate, contribute and achieve.
- A policy for organising and storing materials and equipment should be clearly laid down. Usually, specialist resources will be held centrally, while general materials such as paint and drawing materials are kept distributed around the school.

- There may well be a separate policy statement on assessment to supplement the whole-school policy. Ways of reporting to parents, including appropriate statements, should be explicit; teacher assessment of the subject should be consistent and maintained through portfolio moderation.
- It is important to include a policy statement about information and communication technology (ICT) in relation to Art and Design. This could describe the use of computing as a tool which should be available to students whenever possible.
- Finally, outline the value of display and presentation, indicating when it would be appropriate for pupils to mount and display their own work (see Chapter 7: Developing a creative climate).

The scheme of work

The second section of the documentation should be the scheme of work. It is now recognised that there is more to Art and Design teaching than simply providing the opportunity to explore materials, important though this is. All subject teaching involves progressive planning with clearly identified learning objectives.

To be effective, this document should summarise the programme of activities for Art and Design that will meet the stated objectives for the subject. English schools have, in the past, adopted the NC scheme of work as the basis of their overall programme, but many schools now attempt to define a network of progressive skills, knowledge and understanding that is more integrated with their overall plans or themes to ensure progression and consistency.

There are a number of commercially available schemes claiming to provide all that is needed by busy teachers. As a subject coordinator you might want to critically analyse their assumptions as well as their content. Some staff teams have adopted such schemes as a recipe book of lessons – only to be criticised by visiting inspectors for unimaginative over-reliance on scripts, limiting the creative potential of their pupils.

How, then, can you plan successfully?

Art and Design in our school

To check that the aims of the policy accurately reflect practice in the school, ask all staff this simple question in a development meeting: What do we want to achieve through the delivery of Art or Design in our school? There is certain to be a wide-ranging debate, but it might be wise to ask other Art and Design coordinators how they would steer the discussion to get the most constructive and useful answers!

Using the stated aims of both Early Years Foundation Stage (EYFS – below age 5) and NC documents, a discussion could be steering towards identifying the differences between this (the statutory curriculum) and the aspirations of the school.

This enriching discussion will allow the subject coordinator to assist with the definition of 'the school curriculum' which will need to be published on the school's website. By drawing on the stated aims, it should be possible to review the content of the curriculum offered across the school and ensure the scheme of work encapsulates the intentions and aspirations.

A structure for the plan

There is no single, accepted structure for a scheme of work, but a helpful beginning could be to divide the Art and Design curriculum into two areas. Thus:

Processes	Visual elements
Drawing	Line
Collage	Tone
Painting	Texture
Printing	Colour
Digital media	Pattern
Three-dimensional modelling	Shape
Three-dimensional construction	Three-dimensional form

You should identify the skills and knowledge you want pupils to acquire in each year group, listing the learning objectives for the processes described above, with a separate, though interactive, plan for the visual elements.

Introducing pupils to different artists, designers and craftspeople, whose work centres on a particular process or aspect of the elements, is a useful strategy to ensure that children's studies are based on learning from artists and designers and their work, and that this is integrated systematically. In order to avoid repetition of a narrow range of styles of Art and Design or artists, craftspeople and designers, you must provide a map across the different year groups, so that there is an appropriate and balanced range of genre.

This could be, for example, landscape, portrait, still life, abstract and so on, based around a range of artists of both genders, and work from a range of different periods and cultures.

An Art scheme of work plan is essentially a detailed account of what should take place in each year, and the skills and knowledge that will be acquired. Staff should have the flexibility to deliver this programme of artistic learning through any chosen subject matter and whatever lesson topic they wish, through both subject-centred teaching and cross-curricular activities, as long as they are addressing the learning objectives in the scheme of work.

If you find out about forthcoming exhibitions and opportunities, these can be linked in to the school's medium-term plans.

Breadth, balance, continuity and progression

The Art and Design curriculum content should be broad and balanced, and the programme that you plan should show evidence of continuity and progression, with a wide range of experiences. It is not simply a list of themes and topics, but this can create a dilemma. Perhaps the simple solution would be to identify the constituents of a broad course.

Pupils should be able to:

- engage in observational work and record these observations
- explore sources for imaginative work and personal expression
- develop their Art and Design vocabulary
- evaluate their own and others' artistic endeavours, and, in doing so, develop critical abilities and cultural knowledge
- develop and master a range of processes, media and technologies.

Do remember that many of the activities will be interactive and therefore several processes and objectives are covered simultaneously. For instance, in doing an observational drawing, pupils could learn about the properties of materials, explore the visual elements of line and tone, and develop their Art vocabulary. Your curriculum plan will need to indicate when these aspects need to be addressed separately.

The most challenging aspect of curriculum planning is to identify sequential activities in Art and Design. Some subjects have clear linear progression, as in Mathematics; however in Art and Design it is less clearly defined, because activities are revisited and reinforced in a flexible manner as a 'spiral curriculum'. Nonetheless, a progressive programme of activities can be established. For example:

- Progression is easiest to establish in relation to materials and media and related tools, because most primary teachers recognise that some artistic media are simpler to use than others. Powder paint may be used by all year groups to encourage colour mixing from a dry medium, but exploiting the properties and subtlety of watercolour is more likely to be focused on older primary pupils. Pupils of all ages would use pencils, but the subtle differences that can be gained by using pencils of a range of softness might be most appropriately introduced as children mature. Therefore, although any pupil can use most media and tools at any time, the curriculum planner must decide at what stage pupils can most effectively exploit the potential for learning specific objectives.

- Processes can become more complex as children progress and gain confidence. For instance, vegetable printing and printing from recycled materials are likely to be an Early Years' (below age 5) activity, but screen-printing or printing from compressed polystyrene might be considered more appropriate for older children, when pupils' confidence and their physical skills have increased. However, there is no obvious progression in subject matter. Adventurous teachers now introduce complex issues and themes (such as climate change and environmental issues) to very young pupils with considerable impact and success.

Unless you are the only teacher in the school involved in Art and Design, a scheme of work is essential to avoid overlap and repetition and to provide visible evidence of each individual's progress. What can and will be taught will vary according to the context of the school.

However there will need to be agreement among the staff in a large school as to what is to be taught, in order to ensure that certain Art and Design topics are not repeated too often.

Further guidance

When your scheme of work is produced, some staff will inevitably feel that their own knowledge is too limited to teach some of its aspects effectively: the further guidance section, giving advice about materials and processes, will then be a valuable resource for them.

Part 2 of this book offers a basic compendium of information that you could use for this purpose. There may also be information you would like to include about available shared resources, for example, or you could include a bank of topic-related activities, or possibly images of artists' and designers' work.

This third section of the documents could therefore become quite extensive and, therefore, bulky. It is important to avoid confusion by separating this practical part of guidance from the two previous sections. Many subject coordinators achieve this by putting the policy and scheme of work into their own Subject Coordinator's File, or together with other whole-school policy documents, and leaving the further guidance section available for teachers to access easily, perhaps in the staff room or maybe on the shared drive of the school's computer.

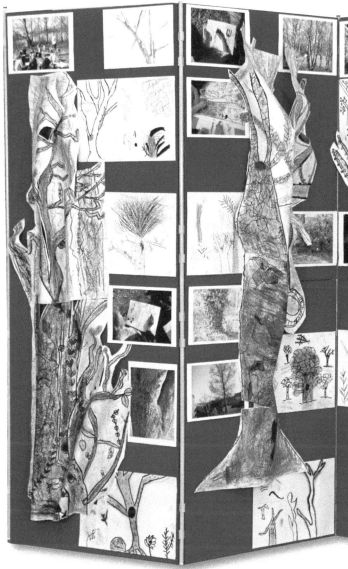

Developing a scheme of work – a whole-school strategy

Curriculum development involves changing accepted working practices, and you could encounter resistance from colleagues who have an established pattern of work. When you develop a scheme of work it is important to build on existing good school practice and ensure ownership by involving all staff in its development. Therefore it is wise to commence with an audit.

Ask all staff to write down what activities in Art and Design took place in their class during the last year, noting the medium used, the skills learned, the visual elements focused upon and aspects of Art history or critical studies that have been addressed. This will be a retrospective record and may require reference to weekly planning.

After everyone has completed this audit, enter the responses on one large-scale grid for collective scrutiny. If the same media/processes, concepts, elements or artistic styles and genres have been offered in different year groups, this repetition will be evident. Ascertain the reason for this. Do activities differ in level or challenge, are they revisited for reinforcement or are they simply being repeated at an individual's whim? A staff meeting is the best place to analyse this in order to reach conclusions about necessary changes to the existing scheme of work. Discussions with the school leadership team will be required if you feel that additional investment in materials or resources is warranted.

Staff development activity

6 Recording progress

Some people believe that Art and Design cannot be assessed as there are no right and wrong answers. Instead, what teachers need to look for is evidence of development in new skills, knowledge and understanding. By creating their own sketchbooks and portfolios, children can self-assess with real evidence of the progress they have made. Art and Design assessment procedures in primary schools are often underdeveloped, providing little indication of the progress actually made by pupils. The reasons for this are discussed in this chapter and suggestions offered to guide a subject coordinator towards establishing a manageable assessment system.

Assessment

How often have you heard teachers say that 'Art and Design cannot be assessed'? However there are aspects of Art and Design that do have a right or wrong response. For example, green is always produced by mixing blue and yellow, and there are facts in Art and Design history that can be remembered and tested.

What these teachers are referring to, of course, is the problem of assessing outcomes of the creative process. Artistic activity cannot be measured in absolute terms and this can lead to the view that Art and Design cannot be assessed at all. However, established sophisticated procedures do exist for assessing pupil achievement, although not in the same way in which achievement in more knowledge-based subjects is evaluated.

Assessment processes must reflect decisions about what is being taught and why. If teachers assess finished work, such as a set of drawings, to check observational accuracy only, the judgement will have little value if the teaching had, for example, focused on developing tone through blending and shading. Instead, you will want to encourage the staff team to understand and apply different assessment forms and processes depending on what is being assessed. You will also want them to see developmental work.

Over-emphasis on certain forms of work (observational studies, for example) can be at the expense of more imaginative and exciting activities. In some cases this can even stop pupils taking risks, which is an important part of any learning process. This is an assessment dilemma, which has parallels in teachers 'teaching to the test' in Literacy activities.

There is much that could be done to make assessment more systematic. However, the wise subject coordinator should be wary of establishing an assessment-driven Art and Design curriculum that restricts the breadth of curriculum experience.

Group assessments

Assessment can develop a knowledge, skills and understanding of Art and Design, especially if learners are actively involved in the process. An atmosphere where pupils enjoy thinking about their own work, and that of their peers, will lead to good quality peer assessment.

Encourage the re-visiting of learning objectives, so pupils' comments can move beyond just 'liking' the work of others. Pupils will then make more reflective comments, building a culture of constructive criticism.

A climate of encouragement and support will help to develop pupils' planning for future improvement.

Strategies for assessment

The most straightforward form of assessment is observation, which reveals a great deal about a child's ability and attitude, and enables you to make a decision about whether to stay quiet, question, or suggest ways of moving forward. You might use the example set by many Early Years' (below age 5) practitioners who use digital photography or video to record children working, or write on sticky notes to capture achievement or effort. Older pupils should be encouraged to take their own photographs and add them to their sketchbooks or other portfolio records, with reflective comments, by way of self-assessment. Other forms of assessment such as holding a life-drawing exercise each year can be useful, although it needs imaginative presentation, as an annual exercise could lack creative excitement.

Portfolios

The subject coordinator should collect a broad selection of pupils' work throughout the year to build up a representative portfolio. This will create interest and excitement, demonstrate what pupils are doing, and show both pupils and staff the standard of work you are expecting. Pupils can be encouraged to construct their own e-portfolio by taking photographs recording their work and processes year-on-year. The e-portfolios can be saved to a portable form, which may then be passed to the secondary school on transition as a helpful record of the children's experience in Art and Design, and the progress and attainment they have made.

A practical policy

Apart from aspects of absolute artistic knowledge, such as factual Art and Design history, all other assessments in Art and Design have to involve judgement.

If clear criteria are agreed, a teacher can make judgements using these benchmarks which, although they are subjective, can generate through moderation procedures with a surprising degree of consensus.

As subject coordinator, you must organise practical assessment procedures with clearly established criteria. These should be published in the school's staff Art and Design policy statement and used throughout the school, and for reporting to parents. The assessment criteria that will be especially useful will allow you and your staff to make the most of key aspects of good Art and Design practice in the classroom. It can be helpful to think in terms of your own questions when you are either observing or in dialogue with pupils to ascertain their level of development, confidence, competence and understanding. Such questions might include examples such as:

- Does the pupil investigate materials and use them experimentally?
- Is the pupil aware of elements of Art, for example line or tone, and apply these to their practical work?
- Can the pupil articulate concepts behind the artwork they have created?
- What degree of detail does the pupil apply to observing a source and recording this visually?

Pupil voice – self-assessment

Effective assessment in Art and Design must take place sensitively, by the teacher discussing with pupils what they have achieved. Written comments are often better than inscrutable marks or grades.

Teachers can help children set their own targets for development and improvement in the same way as for more academic subjects, and pupils may participate in their own assessment if the subject coordinator breaks down their scheme of work into what pupils should know and be able to do. When they agree with the teacher that the standard has been reached, they can check it off on their self-assessment sheet.

Joint assessment between pupils is also invaluable: at key points in a project they can be asked to decide in pairs the best feature of each other's work, explaining what they would do to improve it if it were their own.

Make a portfolio of pupils' work

Generate interest in assessment by gathering a folder of work from across the school and bringing it to a staff meeting or, alternatively, ask everyone to bring examples of children's work. Set up discussion groups and ask teachers to decide whether the work is below, in line with or above a particular level of expectation, as determined by the scheme of work. Encourage teachers to think about how they make judgements about children's work and help them to try to find consensus.

Repeating pieces of work during a pupil's primary school career can also be revealing – providing that it is explained properly to pupils. Teachers should not rely on repeating work too often, as this will become tedious and limit creative development. A record of a child's own drawings from Reception to Year 6 is a great leaving gift for them too.

Assessment for learning means sharing learning objectives with pupils and helping them to know and recognise the standards they are aiming for. It involves pupils in peer and self-assessment, provides feedback which enables them to recognise their next steps, promotes confidence that each and every one can improve, and gets both teacher and pupil to review and reflect on assessment information.

7 | Developing a creative climate

One aspect of your policy may deal with display and presentation but this is only one dimension of a much broader issue. By giving priority to the overall quality of the school's visual environment you could make a significant step towards your goal of raising the status of Art and Design in your school. Visitors can sense a good school from the very moment that they walk through the front entrance by its welcoming displays. Hence, a display policy should not be seen in isolation as it is very much a marker of your school's creative climate.

How effective is your visual appeal?

As subject coordinator you need to look at the overall visual impact of the school. Go outside the school and re-enter as if you were a visitor arriving for the first time. Then ask yourself the following questions:

- How is visual material presented in the hall, corridors and in every classroom?
- Is it changed frequently?
- Are fixtures and fittings well maintained and clean and has furniture been arranged to encourage flexible learning?
- Can pupils access learning materials easily and independently?

Visitors will begin to draw their conclusions from the care and consistency that has been taken with presentation, and, importantly, so will the pupils. Children's visual education is continually operating throughout the school environment, which, if managed effectively, becomes a practical example of the principles of good visual design.

You may ask why this is the specific concern of the hard-pressed Art and Design subject coordinator, particularly if it is not explicit in your job description. It is because the person charged with establishing and maintaining the creative climate is the person who is by definition most visually aware. The buck may stop with you, so see this as an opportunity to raise the status of the subject you lead, and make sure it is a key strand in your development plan.

A consistent approach

Establishing a specific display policy can be surprisingly problematic. It can become a contentious issue within a school, especially when you would like everyone to adopt it. This is because teachers tend to divide into two camps, with the views of the most extreme in each one being difficult to reconcile. On the one hand, some extremists believe that every school should have an absolutely clear set of rules for the organisation of stimulus and presentation of pupils' work, which is adhered to by everyone, so that there is absolute consistency across the school. On the other hand, at the other end of the spectrum, is a conviction that to be told exactly how to display work in their classroom represents a violation of human rights.

The problems arise because, as in most aesthetic choices, there is no absolute right and wrong; the same lively display created by one person is in another's eyes muddled and messy. One teacher's carefully discreet choice of mounting paper is to another simply 'dull and boring'. When a person's taste is questioned or when, even worse, they are not permitted to exercise their personal choice because it is not in line with agreed practice, they can lose heart or even become disgruntled. Failing to meet this challenge can create a visual free for all that results in a chaotic jumble.

So do not underestimate the pitfalls if you are asked to reconcile these opposing viewpoints, but rise to the challenge nevertheless. Maybe somewhere halfway along the continuum is the most secure position for the wise subject coordinator to establish their initial position.

Your display policy

It should now be clear that it is better to take a broad view when attempting to influence a creative climate policy for the school, and one aspect of this will involve setting some standards and procedures for display. There are likely to be some basic principles that everyone should be willing to sign up to initially, before focusing on the more specific aspects of display.

Stimulus displays

No one would argue against consistent systems for organising resources and equipment throughout the school, as these will facilitate easy transfer from one class to another. Equally, no teacher would suggest that schools should not be visually stimulating places. It should therefore be easy to suggest that every classroom has a range of exciting visual stimuli related to a particular topic and displayed in an inventive manner. You can argue that displaying the most ordinary objects in a new way, outside their normal environment, will draw attention to them and increase children's visual literacy and awareness. You can further suggest allowing children to handle objects, so that they can explore tactile as well as visual qualities. Logically, the outcomes of any pupils' work using these stimuli should be displayed alongside the artefacts in a way that enhances their creative efforts.

Choosing what to display

In displaying pupils' work, another controversial issue may arise. Which pupils' work is displayed?

If only the 'best' work is put up (which is tempting as this will provide examples of best practice for others to emulate) some pupils will be disadvantaged, so all staff need to agree that it is important that each child has some of their achievements celebrated publicly.

It may also be useful to demonstrate during a staff workshop how to mount children's work to give it added status.

What goes on display is another important issue to be addressed in your policy. Most teachers will recognise that too much dense written work is visually unappealing and children will not look at it, so encourage your colleagues to choose a few choice quotations as a preferable option. In the same way, too much work crammed into one small display space is confusing, so use your policy to suggest that teachers spread displays over two or more boards to provide visual relief.

Refreshing regularly

No one would challenge the view that unless displays are changed regularly they become part of the wallpaper – even time-consuming impressive ones. Your policy can explain that displays reflect current work, and should be changed and updated at least every term.

You should not find it difficult persuading teachers to accept these and other broad principles, if they can then have individual freedom to display work in their classrooms. You could then create a whole-school visual harmony in common areas, such as corridors and the entrance hall.

Your ambitions may be even greater and this is where each subject coordinator, who knows their staff well, will also know how far they can go.

Providing guidelines

Remember that the head teacher of the school is also likely to have a view about how corporate a display policy should be and whether this is enforced at the expense of individual flexibility, so they should also be involved in planning your display policy.

Taking the head teacher along with you in your development plan has been the strategy so far – and it is still important here. Whatever you eventually agree in your school should be written up as a basic policy, with a set of advice and guidelines that can be added to your documentation as an appendix.

Leading by example

The best way to inspire other teachers to develop their own interesting and creative displays is to lead by example.

The following are a few simple guidelines which you can use and then, once you are confident in these basic principles, you might wish to experiment further.

- **Colours** The colours in the children's work should dictate the colour of the mount and the display background. Take care that the background colour complements the pupils' work rather than fighting with it. Soft toned greys and beige papers, or strong black and whites are often good choices as these look good behind almost anything. If you do want to use a colour mount, pick up a subtle colour theme from the pupils' work, rather than obtrusive mounts in vivid ones.

- **Mounting** It must first be decided whether all pieces of work should be mounted.
  All work that is displayed in the classroom deserves to be presented with care, although the extreme of 'double mounting' every piece of work is time-consuming and does not fit in with resource shortages. Not all work needs to be mounted; for example, it would not be sensible to back large artwork or ephemeral pieces.

- **Cutting** You should aim for about a centimetre border all the way around on your mount. This gives a sense of consistency even if the pieces of work are different sizes. Think carefully before displaying work at an angle, as this can be distracting.

- **Positioning** Fitting several items onto a rectangular display board is another problem. When displaying a number of pieces of work, your job becomes much simpler if you begin with the first piece right in the centre and work outwards, creating vertical, horizontal and diagonal designs. When you stand, away from the board, you will see a harmonious arrangement that you can be proud of. Put just one staple loosely into each piece until you are happy with the display, as this will give you flexibility to move things around easily. Remember children's eye levels when you put up a display, as small children will find it difficult to see if it is too high.

- **Originality** Eventually, you will want to become more creative and original. Do look at shop windows for inspiration and ideas, but do not fall into the trap of thinking that children's work has to look that perfect.

- **Attaching** All this work needs to be fastened securely to the board, and a staple-gun is a good tool for the job, as the staples are less visible than drawing pins, which can create a spotty, visually disturbing effect. It is a good idea to insert the staples at an angle, so they are easier to remove when taking down the display.

- **Lettering** Lettering for the display is important and, using ICT, simple straightforward captions can be produced easily. Lettering styles should be simple and consistent throughout a display, although freehand lettering can be used where appropriate. Some would say this is an opportunity to show pupils an example of handwriting. If a display is to be more than just a way of enhancing work or decorating the school, it should challenge the viewer. Display titles that ask questions are preferable to simply describing the content. For example, 'How many different greens can you see in these pictures by Class Two?' If creative work has been inspired by stimulus material, display it alongside to make the context meaningful.

- **Three-dimensional work** To display three-dimensional work you need to find and create special spaces. Extend lengths of fabric from a wall display onto boxes or tables to change from the vertical to the horizontal. The principles already mentioned apply equally to three-dimensional as two-dimensional displays.

Too many objects create a cluttered effect that looks disorganised in a small classroom. Displaying three-dimensional works from the ceiling is possible, although some security systems which are sensitive to movement can make this problematic. Corners and windowsills are useful places for three-demensional displays, as they are less obstructive to everyday activity.

Reflection

A positive and beautiful learning environment can make all the difference to help motivate and assist pupils in feeling welcomed and valued. Staff can also learn to enjoy expressing their own creativity through making displays; although it is important that the display policy is introduced tactfully. There needs to be open discussion and individual negotiations with staff, so that everyone feels they have ownership of the general principles as well as the specific procedures. In this sense the same strategy outlined for establishing the scheme of work should be utilised by the subject coordinator to establish a policy for the school's creative climate.

A school that puts a cohesive policy systematically into practice is not merely adopting a marketing strategy to create a good impression. By actively designing the pupils' environment, their visual education is continually being enhanced.

Staff development activity

Discussing displays

Book a staff meeting to discuss display in your school. Prepare the staff by asking them to walk around the whole school looking at displays before the meeting.

During the meeting organise group discussions and mind-mapping activities to collect teachers' thoughts on what they have seen.

- ▶ What did they like, and what did not work so well?
- ▶ Which areas of the school could be improved by more focused displays?
- ▶ Do all displays reflect current topics and learning?

Ask groups to feed back their discussions to help find some common consent on the features that make a good display.

If you have time, provide a practical activity to finish your meeting, such as a workshop on choosing colours and backgrounds, or by giving pairs a random object and asking them to display it imaginatively in only five minutes.

8 | Art and Design across the curriculum

Literacy and Numeracy are prioritised in the primary curriculum, arguably to the disadvantage of Art and Design. However a subject coordinator can capitalise on this fact by demonstrating that Art and Design contribute to pupils' development across the whole curriculum. In this way, the subject will gain status, even with those who have a degree of scepticism about the value of more expressive activities. Exploiting direct links with Literacy, through the use of sketchbooks and notebooks and Numeracy with patterns and shape is a sensible strategy.

Art, Design and Literacy

Practical activities and collaborative group work naturally encourage children to express ideas and negotiate with one another. This not only extends their vocabulary, but also develops the important social and communication skills that are necessary for progress in all areas of learning.

Sketchbooks contain children's own research and written notes, as well as being a place for recording visual experiences. Many schools encourage the use of sketchbooks as a tool for thinking, or a place for children to document learning across the different curriculum areas.

Because these books are intended for children to collect and develop ideas spontaneously, it would be inappropriate for teachers to mark them in the same way as more formal writing, but they are excellent tools for assessing children's skills in written expression, and key words and grammar can be reinforced as and when it is appropriate.

Encouraging pupils to evaluate the work of mature, possibly famous, artists as well as that of their peers and their own personal creative efforts raises their confidence in forming and articulating their own opinions. It will also, importantly, have a positive impact on their writing skills. This type of critical analysis can take place during a whole-class discussion, small group activities, or when the children work in pairs to discuss work together.

The key point is that pupils get used to expressing their opinions about a range of works of Art. Most importantly, they make aesthetic judgements and are able to give reasons for their choices.

Engaging with artwork

Children should have access to cultural and historical knowledge and understanding (UN Convention for Children's Rights, Article 31). Looking at artefacts and artists' and designers' work from different periods and cultures is a natural way to teach subjects such as History and Geography, and reinforcing this learning with practical Art and Design tasks will bring those lessons to life. In this way cross-cultural understanding can also be increased.

Visual grammar

Children learn that artists and designers often give their work a title, so encourage them to do the same. In every primary classroom art- or design work is likely to be displayed with the name of the young artist who has produced it, mirroring what happens in an Art gallery. As subject coordinator you can also encourage colleagues to label children's work with key words relating to its production. For instance, the aim of the work might be 'exploring the visual element of line'. In this way, pupils' vocabulary will develop in parallel with their visual grammar.

There are many ways that words and pictures can be brought together inventively. For instance, you can give pupils words such as 'smooth', 'rough', 'interconnected' and so on, and ask them to make a response in a medium such as clay. Text can be used within artwork, incising words, names or titles into the surface of pieces that have been cast in plaster before it dries.

Art, Design and Numeracy

The potential for linking Art and Design with Numeracy is enormous. The systematic rhythms and forms of nature and the Earth, and their underlying mathematical structures have proved a rich stimulus for many artists and designers.

For instance, Leonardo da Vinci's sketchbook shows how he evolved some of his mechanical structures from a study of grasses. Introduce older pupils to the 'Golden Section' and Fibonacci, to illustrate the relationship between mathematical sequences and natural forms. Practical activities can include: making tessellation patterns, using large-scale geometric works as a basis for small-scale clay structures; or drawing around large cardboard cut-out circles, squares and triangles to produce dynamic geometric patterns, perhaps after looking at artwork such as that of Frank Stella.

Art, Design and Science

A visit to your local Science museum can be a fantastic starting point for an Art and Design project. A good Art and Design subject coordinator will enjoy exploring an imaginative and inquiry-based approach.

For older and more able pupils consider a project on 'making connections', using their sketchbooks and a digital camera. Challenge them to record both natural forms and phenomena that demonstrate symmetry and repeating patterns, and manufactured structures or objects that replicate patterns from nature. For instance, ripples in water juxtaposed with undulating patterns in roof tiles; the spiral of a shell connected to a spiral staircase; and so on. These sketchbook studies can then be developed into larger works.

Staff development activity

Peer critique

1. A comment and a question
   - ▶ When asking pupils to appraise work, make sure the whole class takes part. This activity is designed for groups of children working collaboratively.
   - ▶ Ask the groups to display their work on the table tops.
   - ▶ Leave sticky notes and pencils in a pot on each table.
   - ▶ Encourage children to look at each other's work, then leave an anonymous note with one comment and one question for the artists.
   - ▶ Children can then go back to their own table to see what their peers thought of their work.
2. A star and a wish
   - ▶ Towards the end of a lesson where pupils have been working independently, ask each pupil to exchange their art- or design work with someone else.
   - ▶ Ask them to each describe what they feel is the best feature of the work, and how they would improve it. As each child is both giving and receiving a critique, sensitive and carefully expressed judgements usually prevail.

9

Part 2 Materials and process
The language of Art and Design: the visual elements

A subject coordinator who has some background of artistic study is likely to have a reasonable understanding of the formal visual elements of Art and Design: line; tone; shape; space; form; texture; pattern and colour. As subject coordinator you will find that not all staff will have even this basic level of knowledge of how images can be constructed, and many teachers will need some support if they are to introduce pupils to the language of Art and Design. The visual elements are an essential tool for developing visual awareness, and your scheme of work should address them. This chapter offers a strategy for their development in your school.

What is visual vocabulary?

The visual vocabulary of Art and Design can be likened to the development of vocabulary in the teaching of language. Any work of visual Art and Design involves the use of different aspects of the visual elements: line; colour; texture; pattern; shape; tone; space; and form.

The origins of this concept can be found in the innovative work of the Bauhaus movement, and was developed by an artist named Maurice de Sausmarez in his book, *Basic Design: The Dynamics of Visual Form* (2nd edition, 2007), which made these educational principles widely accessible in the 1960s. Teachers can make pupils aware of this language during any Art or Design project, which will assist in developing and extending their personal visual vocabulary and help increase the expressive capacity of their work.

Observational sources

The simplest way of introducing primary pupils to the visual elements is to develop their understanding by using a first-hand observational source: this is much better than starting with abstract concepts, as the objective can be kept tighter this way.

The teacher can focus children's attention upon subject matter that provides appropriate challenges for their age and development. For example, children might learn how to represent different surfaces by using a multi-sensory approach: they could explore the textures and forms of a variety of natural objects by touch, and by looking closely with a magnifying glass. They could then use drawing materials to represent changes in surface, perhaps with a focus on light and shade, or pattern and texture, or form and shape. Maybe they might enrich the drawing of a bird by concentrating on ways of representing the soft texture of the feathers – or perhaps they could attempt to mix colours that closely match their observed source.

Recording visual enquiry

It will be helpful to make a sequence of observational drawings concentrating on, for example, linear or tonal qualities of the object in question, and to use a sketchbook to record such visual explorations. Establishing the use of a sketchbook, or visual diary, and using it in part to explore the visual elements is an important way to encourage thinking skills. Remember that a sketchbook should be used as a visual journal rather than a drawing book. This will help children to realise the full potential of enquiry-based learning. There is nothing to stop you creating imaginative formats for sketchbooks in your school, such as using a box to collect items or by keeping virtual sketchbooks, digitally scanned records or blogs (see Chapter 11: Technology and new media).

There are several ways that a sketchbook can be used to help develop children's understanding of visual language.

Pupils can be encouraged to:
- Gather new and exciting source materials to stimulate the development of ideas. For example, they might collect small samples from the environment that focus on particular aspects of the visual elements, such as a dry and brittle autumn leaf, or a weathered piece of paper, as a record of a particular colour or textured feature. These may then be stuck into the sketchbook as part of a reference collection.
- Make collages, for example by collecting wax rubbings from a variety of different surfaces and use these to create interesting, textured collages.
- Make a shape or pattern 'collection' by recording geometric shapes or repeating patterns that they notice in and around their school, home and the local environment.
- Simply experiment with colour and coloured media and materials.
- Make brief visual notes, written comments and annotations.

Pupils should continue to be challenged to find and record in their sketchbook aspects of the visual environment which concentrate on line, colour, pattern and so on, to build up their own personal visual vocabulary reference book.

Visual elements and media

Some visual elements have associations with a particular medium. Non-specialists may find it less confusing and easier to understand if your scheme of work makes suggestions for work with a particular medium alongside an appropriate visual element. For instance, there is a traditional relationship between: drawing and line and tone; painting and colour; printmaking with surface and texture; and clay and other three-dimensional materials with space and form.

Most Art activities, however, involve interaction between some or all of the visual elements. For example: drawings can be coloured; printmaking can make use of line and tone as well as texture and pattern; and a collage could combine aspects of several of the visual elements. Form and space can best be understood through practical activities using three-dimensional materials, although digital and architectural drawings are also good ways to explore these elements.

Planning for progression

Some aspects of learning related to the visual elements involve specific and measurable knowledge and can thus be taught progressively, as already outlined in the section on planning a scheme of work. For instance: pupils need to understand that when two primary colours are mixed a secondary one is made; that there are warm and cold colours; and that complementary colours are strongly contrasting ones which are found as opposite partners on a colour wheel.

Rather than attempting to teach this mechanically, your pupils need to be given the opportunity to experiment with various colour media to discover for themselves the 'rules' of colour, and they should experience producing harmonious or visually dynamic artworks through their own creative process. Ultimately there are no right or wrong answers in such exploratory visual activity once the rules are understood. Just as, for example, pupils learn the rules of grammar to express themselves correctly – although a piece of writing involves originality and creativity which do not adhere to absolute rules.

It is the same in learning visual language, and pupils should be encouraged to evaluate each of their personal efforts critically. Teachers must develop skills in questioning pupils in order to extend their awareness and to encourage further exploration and experimentation. For instance they should ask pupils to look closely at a natural form and describe how many different types of line they can find to draw, using appropriate media to compare thick lines with thin, hard with soft and furry with crisp.

Looking at Art and Design

The visual literacy of children can be further developed by studying the work of other artists, crafts people and designers. Every piece of Art and Design can be appreciated or analysed in terms of the formal visual elements, and some early 20th-century Art and Design was concerned specifically with taking an observed visual starting point and 'abstracting' from it; systematically reducing the observed source to its basic visual elements, so that its origin was sometimes barely or no longer recognisable.

A good example of this is the Cubist movement, where observed information is visually reduced to geometric shapes, split up and then reconstructed into new compositions. For examples look at artists such as Pablo Picasso and Georges Braque.

Some artists, particularly those working in the 1960s, were occupied with manipulating the visual elements to produce an artwork that was visually pleasing and stimulating, without an observed starting point, and thus totally 'abstract' from beginning to end.

These works can be read purely in relation to the visual elements so they provide useful examples in the classroom to discuss qualities of colour, or texture and composition, as a way of extending their understanding of the visual elements. For example, you might look at artists such as Kim MacConnel or Mark Rothko.

An enquiring look at the work of contemporary artists will encourage discussion and help develop a wider understanding of the language of Art and Design. In the 21st century it is not sufficient to interpret works of Art simply by the formal elements alone, for example many contemporary art- or design works rely upon ideas or concepts behind the image to communicate with the audience, for instance by looking at the work of artists such as Martin Creed.

While this is a useful tool to engage children, contextual information gleaned through enquiry will further develop and extend children's visual literacy. An introduction to the work of some key artists from a wide range of cultural and historical sources should be incorporated systematically into the school scheme of work.

Many works of Art and Design, as well as free access to museums and galleries, are available through the internet for use on the interactive whiteboard; although good quality printed reproductions continue to be a valuable resource for classroom use.

Exploring the visual elements

Non-specialist teachers in primary schools may understandably be hesitant about teaching the language of Art and Design and leading class discussions on artists' and designers' work. It is important to recognise that the best way to develop staff skills is through personal engagement in practical activities.

Plan strategic in-service training sessions, or staff meetings, which focus on using media to explore the visual elements. Examples might include: using charcoal and chalk to investigate line and tone; paint or pastels to explore colour; and clay to express form.

Why not be even more innovative and have an inspirational staff Inset day in an art gallery? One of the gallery's education officers will help you get the most from your visit.

On your return to school you can encourage all staff to use art- and design works as a matter of routine, perhaps linking them to topic work, in order to develop children's visual literacy in a more integrated and natural way. For example, you might encourage teachers to devote a classroom display board to an 'Artwork of the Month'. The purpose of which is to promote discussion and to emphasise key artistic terms and language that children can use within their own visual responses.

10 | Learning from artists and designers

Art activities in primary schools are predominantly practical and this approach is based on the philosophy of writers such as Herbert Read, whose model for Art education was the 'child as artist'. This does not mean that every child is a potential professional but it reminds us to try to keep the confidence and enthusiasm that children have for Art and Design. In fact only a small number of your pupils are likely to study at Art school and even fewer will become professional artists or designers. However the great majority will be consumers of Art and Design in their adult lives and so learning from artists and designers has become a regular feature of Art and Design education in schools.

Appreciating Art and Design

Although personal growth is one key aim of Art and Design education, it must also educate pupils to make informed aesthetic choices in life, for example appreciating Art and Design, and making fashion choices and Design decisions. This can happen through actually doing Art and Design, but a number of major Art and Design educators, such as Elliot Eisner, have questioned the extent to which a purely practical Art and Design programme can effectively develop pupils' 'critical and cultural abilities'. In England every version of the NC has contained references to the importance for pupils' learning about artists, their work and applying this understanding to developing their own knowledge and skills. It is now generally accepted that a teacher ought to provide experiences to help develop the pupils' visual awareness.

Pupils should be encouraged to explore relationships between their own 'making' practice and their appreciation and knowledge of established works of Art, Craft and Design. As subject coordinator you will want to address this and allow good learning opportunities to be developed.

This may not seem a problem to someone with an Art and Design background, but a less experienced teacher can find the challenge daunting. As a consequence, such teachers tend to choose safe and easily accessible sources to study. For instance, it is common to find children making a self-portrait influenced by Pablo Picasso, exploring optical colour mixing by looking at Georges Seurat, or using Paul Klee's stylised fish as a basis for collage work or looking at the patterns created by William Morris as a basis for Design work. These examples may be typical of the range of mature artists and designers often used in primary schools – but such a range should be seen as rather narrow.

It is understandable that non-Art and Design specialist teachers want to use art- and design works that they personally enjoy and are familiar with, but the subject coordinator must check that there is not an over-concentration on the same artists and designers. The programme should be broad and balanced, covering a wide range of artists and designers from different genres, periods and cultures, with no gender bias.

Talking about Art

Children should talk about artists, designers, and art- and design works, and the making of Art and Design. They should be encouraged to express a balanced and reasoned opinion, and recognise that there are alternative perspectives.

Children may make immediate arbitrary choices about what they like and dislike about a work of Art or Design. These opinions are of course entirely valid, but their judgements have not necessarily involved high-order thinking skills or the application of aesthetic values. A framework for deeper analysis can be developed by the teacher through skilful questioning. How has the artist or designer used their chosen medium? Which visual elements are evident? Do children think there is a message communicated by the work of Art? These types of questions can produce a debate in class.

Critical thinking

As subject coordinator you might organise an activity for a staff meeting or training day based on analysing art- or design work. Teachers should develop confidence in making a balanced aesthetic evaluation of a variety of art- or design works, which they can then use across the whole curriculum. Teachers should recognise that the aim of introducing artists' and designers' work is not to 'educate' pupils into the good taste of the teacher, but to encourage children to think for themselves.

The most appropriate teaching style is, therefore, interactive and informal. Presenting artists' and designers' work as an Art and Design history talk is not usually helpful as it can become overly knowledge-based, disadvantaging some children and causing others to disengage entirely.

Learning from artworks

The teacher's role is to help children understand the relationship between their own practical work and their appreciation and knowledge of established works of Art, Craft and Design. This is crucially important: works of Art, Craft and Design should stimulate ideas and discussion, but children can also be encouraged to interpret them visually. You don't simply have to copy.

Consider making a three-dimensional version of a two-dimensional image in a material such as clay, or turn an original drawing into a three-dimensional form 'hanging' suspended from the ceiling. Extend pupils' use of media by studying the way an artist has applied paint, or explore the visual elements through a study of an artist or designer by adopting their chosen colour scheme.

Every general primary topic will provide an opportunity for some related practical work. A project on bicycles could feature Fernand Léger and Jean Metzinger; a sea theme could produce a three-dimensional octopus after looking at the work of Utagawa Kuniyoshi and Kawanabe Kyosai; or you could help pupils work from digital photographs of themselves asleep in deckchairs in the style of Beryl Cook. A transport project could look at the Futurists or Tony Cragg's towers made from cars; the theme of water might lead to experimentation with the way that Helen Frankenthaler poured thin veils of colour onto raw canvas. Or a topic on Ancient Greece might give rise for an opportunity to make a large-scale relief collage after studying the Elgin Parthenon frieze.

Avoid direct copying

Basing pupils' practical work on the work of mature artists and designers doesn't have to mean, for example, copying a reproduction of Vincent Van Gogh's painting of sunflowers. Instead, teachers could discuss his use of colour, and possibly ask pupils to experiment with some of the ways in which he applied paint or laid certain colours next to one another. This could be done in pupils' sketchbooks, before returning to first-hand observation of sunflowers, set up perhaps as a Van Gogh still life for a large-scale practical activity. There are limitless approaches that avoid direct copying.

Resources

As the subject coordinator you will need to develop a large bank of visual resources. One of the reasons why a narrow range of artists is often presented to pupils is that resources are limited. There should be enough resources for whole-class teaching, and donated original works would be a huge bonus. Most classrooms have access to data projectors, interactive whiteboards and so on to share Art and Design from galleries around the world, but it is also important to work with reproductions which children can study closely and handle. Purchasing new resources from allocated funds should feature as a regular strand in your development plan.

The selection of resources should be as wide as possible. Reproductions can be kept in plastic wallets to withstand wear from use, and are best kept centrally; the subject coordinator will also need to establish a system to track them once borrowed. There are many websites providing examples of the work and it will help busy colleagues if the further guidance section of your documentation (see Chapter 5: Planning for Art and Design) includes specific references for these.

Artists and designers in school

Inviting artists and designers into school can stimulate exciting Art and Design activity, but remember that they are not supply teachers. Be absolutely clear about what you want to achieve, and consult staff to ensure that they develop a sense of partnership with the artist or designer. An artist's or designer's work with pupils should focus on 'de-coding' their own practice.

Talk to the artist or designer in advance about children's previous experience and make sure that materials are available for the session. They may not be familiar with the normal rhythms of the school day nor be a natural communicator with children, so preparation and planning are vital if such events are to be successful. There may be funding opportunities available to help with artist and designer placements. Part of your role will be to explore and utilise these.

Using Art galleries

Visiting exhibitions in a local gallery can also be a source of inspiration for primary pupils, although it should not replace ongoing work in the classroom initiated by the teacher's medium-term planning.

Teachers should always visit the gallery themselves before taking pupils there, partly to undertake a necessary risk assessment, but also, importantly, to plan the learning opportunities so that nothing is left to chance. Some contemporary Art and Design, for example, is aimed to shock or provoke audiences, so professional judgement will be needed in deciding whether an exhibition is appropriate or not. If in doubt, invite another teacher to visit the exhibition with you.

Many galleries organise events for teachers to see new exhibitions often for free and after hours. These events can be a good opportunity to discuss with colleagues the exhibition. Larger galleries may also publish special teacher's packs of resources to develop activities in school, and many of these are available online. Registering to receive information about forthcoming exhibitions will mean you have time to think about which artists and designers to include in the scheme of work for the year ahead.

Some teachers have found visits to exhibitions with pupils especially helpful if they are planning to set up an exhibition for parents and visitors in the school. Aspects of gallery exhibition such as layout, use of lighting, design and information provided by notices and catalogues, the role of the guides and so on can all be adapted in school with careful planning.

Staff development activity

Visiting galleries

As subject coordinator, you will want to ensure that artists' work is presented to pupils in a meaningful way. Devoting a complete training day to taking the staff to visit a gallery can be an enlightening and inspiring experience.

You should be able to ask the gallery's education officer to speak to your group to explain what the gallery has to offer for schools. You can then suggest that teachers build gallery visits into their planning as part of their annual routine. It is important that these visits are not seen as isolated 'day trips' but that they are followed up with related practical activity back in the classroom. Children should be able to apply the knowledge and understanding they have gained, from looking at the real thing, into their own artwork. Teachers will be able to assess the impact of visiting a gallery on the pupils' responses and outcomes.

A challenge for many teachers lies in the realm of contemporary Art and Design: you can support them by ensuring that there is a wide variety of images available, perhaps topic related, for teachers to choose from and use in the classroom.

Think about buying some picture frames, in which pieces of Art or Design can be displayed around the school. Regularly change the prints and samples, so that you have your own art gallery.

11 | Technology and new media

Technological equipment and processes are developing faster than ever and primary school children are sometimes more familiar with them than their teachers. As subject coordinator for Art and Design it will be an essential part of your plan to make sure that ICT and new media are embedded and exploited throughout the Art and Design curriculum. Supporting staff in experimenting with new media alongside children in their class will update skills and enrich learning for all. However, make sure there is a well-researched policy for using technology in the school to ensure pupils' safety.

Art and Design practice

Many contemporary artists and designers use digital technology as an integral part of their Art and Design practice, whether in the formation and development of an initial idea, or through one of the designing stages, or in the presentation of the final outcome for a public audience. Of course schools should reflect the fact that this practice is now common and digital technology should be given as much status and time in classes as traditional techniques.

The pace of innovation in the digital world is hard to keep up with and it is worth remembering that children in your school will grow up to enter a world that we cannot currently imagine. It is therefore important to provide opportunities for them to use a range of equipment, not only for research purposes, but also to explore and experiment with in their own way. It is worth creating a list of artists and designers who use digital techniques and include this in your scheme of work appendix to help support teachers who are not familiar with this area of Art and Design media. Look, for example, on the internet at the work of Greyworld: the piece entitled *Paint* (2010) is a great place to start.

Collaboration and a creative approach

Due to time and curriculum pressures, teachers are often expected to learn how to use digital equipment in their own time. You might find that some staff have an intuitive approach to picking up new techniques and adapting already known ones, and they will do this with ease. Other teachers might lack skills and confidence, and this is made even worse by the fact that many children are very computer literate.

A subject coordinator should find out sensitively which teachers need extra help and focus support on them. You should already have your suspicions from the audit (Appendix 2: Subject coordinator's staff questionnaire) that you asked them to complete.

Equipment and techniques

As subject coordinator, it is important to research any major new purchases. Many schools have invested in ICT equipment which has quickly become out of date. Class computers, communal computer suites and portable laptops are commonplace in most primary schools, and in Art and Design pupils will frequently use these for research, creating digital drawings or paintings and for designing. Cameras and video cameras are also basic classroom equipment. Only a few years ago there might have been one digital camera locked away for special occasions, but now most teachers have access at least to a class camera. In some schools, and this is particularly true in some Early Years' (below age 5) classes, children have general access to cameras and can use them as a tool for discovery and recording, just as they might use a pencil or paper. This is very good practice as it reinforces creative and independent learning, and you might consider this for every class, perhaps as a target in your long- or medium-term vision for the subject. Interactive whiteboards and internet access in classrooms means that pupils can be introduced to galleries and Art and Design works from all around the world at the press of a key.

Digital photography

There are plenty of valuable reasons for including photography in daily classroom activity. It can give children the opportunity to be innovative and they can use this tool for communicating their ideas, thoughts and feelings. Some young children will own or have used a mobile phone with a camera facility, and there are digital cameras specially designed for the youngest of children. Whether children have experience of using cameras or not, all expensive, shared equipment needs respect and it is important that children understand how to look after it and use it correctly. This is a lesson that will be worth revisiting at the beginning of each academic year or new photography project.

Once pupils have grasped the basic camera functions, teach them how to use the zoom function to create close-ups and explore texture and detail.

Show them how to make use of different viewpoints by placing the camera at ground level and taking insect-view shots, or by pointing the camera upwards to create long shots. Take the opportunity to teach them about structure in composition, colour, and how to create mood and atmosphere with light and tone. An understanding of the visual elements will come into play when making decisions about taking photographs and, with digital photography, the delete function means that pupils can experiment without feeling inhibited.

If children are confident with cameras and are accessing them independently, much of this artistic understanding of how to get the best out of a photograph will be transferred to other curriculum areas, such as Science, History or Geography, as well as photo-documentation during school trips and visits.

Pupils should also be encouraged to document their own art- and design work as it progresses and upload pictures to the school website or an online gallery or photo-sharing site. Don't forget that if pupils are uploading images of themselves and their friends, you must have parents' permission. A standard form that parents sign at the beginning of the school year usually covers this, but it is very important to check your school's policy.

Digital tablets

Tablets are now frequently used in primary schools and can be very useful because of the intuitive nature of the device. The touch screen function is one that pupils are very familiar with in their everyday lives, and applying specifically designed apps for drawing, painting and even for exploring form through three-dimensional graphics, can be akin to more traditional activities such as finger-painting and sketching, so special pen-like tools are available for fine and detailed work. These devices can also be used for photography and video work, and the screen size makes them easy for younger pupils to use. Pupils can learn about layers, transparency and opacity, zooming in and out, and cropping in order to make decisive compositions. Pupils can experiment freely by combining text, sound and images to express their ideas and create new work, and they can learn how to save and share their work as well. The internet facility makes this tool an ideal one-stop shop for creating artworks and graphic designing digitally. Their work can be saved to online storage facilities or it can be uploaded to an online children's gallery site, for example Artsonia. The tablet requires minimal technical support so teachers can be free to teach rather than having to run around a computer suite sorting out hitches. You will need to check that internet sites you wish to use are permitted in your school, as some will be automatically barred from use.

Blogging

If carefully introduced, blogging will allow pupils to be publishers of their own work and develop a sense of themselves as artists and designers, sharing their work with a wider audience. One class blog can be created and monitored so that all children can add to one stream: this enables topic-based work to be developed in a collaborative way, very much like a virtual 'working wall'. The blog can be shared internally with other classes, or you might connect with schools internationally through sites such as Global Gateway.

A blog may also be seen as a virtual sketchbook, or visual diary, and this can be a personal space in which pupils may upload short paragraphs of text, video footage, photographs and so on onto a simple webpage, and the blog posts will accumulate in chronological order. A blog will also invite responses in the form of posts from other children, so feedback is generated and a dialogue begins between the participating children.

Willingness to engage in dialogue and reflect upon feedback are essential elements of generally progressing well, not only in Art and Design, and this is a life skill which tomorrow's generation will need more than ever.

Film and video

If you visit a contemporary Art gallery, you cannot fail to notice that video and film are widely accepted as Art forms and, if you have the equipment available, using this medium can be an exciting and motivating project for any age group. As well as creating short dramas or visual pieces for installation work, children can be introduced to animation techniques using drawings or model making, and create short films in this way, too.

All film work needs children to work in teams and the wider benefits are that they learn to negotiate and cooperate to achieve an outcome that they can celebrate together.

Most computers will have film-making software already installed, and there are many commercial animation software programs that are simple to use and available to buy relatively cheaply.

Encourage teachers to introduce artists and designers who use digital techniques. Include a list of these with website information in your curriculum plan appendix.

Internet safety is vital

If you are encouraging staff in your school to use technology, such as the internet, for sharing images, you must also be sure the school has an updated policy on internet safety. Look at the current guidelines on internet safety available from government websites.

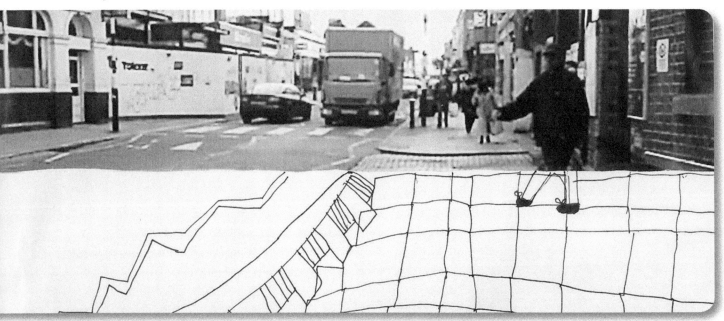

Staff development activity

Using new technology

It is a good idea to introduce new equipment to everyone at the same time, in a non-threatening atmosphere. For example you might demonstrate the key features of a tablet computer during a staff meeting and you can then encourage teachers to see what they can do with it, even play 'games' if necessary, to help them familiarise themselves. If teachers lack confidence with new technology, suggest that they engage their children in ICT through Art and Design. This approach requires teachers to back off from direct, front of class teaching and allows the children to take a more proactive position in which they can share knowledge and discoveries. The teacher will need to be open-minded enough to learn from the children who will be excited to be able to demonstrate their understanding. As subject coordinator, your job is to nurture a collaborative learning environment in which everyone, both pupils and staff, are the learners. Don't forget to keep your own skills and knowledge up to date too.

If you are looking for inspiration or to find out about the very latest digital technology innovations, you might look at the TED Talks online website (TED stands for Technology, Entertainment, Design). Search for artists' or designers' talks – and prepare to be amazed.

12 | Drawing

Many artists and Art and Design educators regard drawing as a particularly important activity, yet it is the one that many non-specialists regard as the most difficult to teach. This is often because teachers feel they lack necessary expertise in their own skills. It can also be due to misconceptions of what successful drawing actually is, and the belief that to create a 'good' drawing children should produce a 'correct' observational representation.

Taking a broader view with regard to the function of drawing, for example as an act of exploration as well as the recording of something, can increase teachers' confidence significantly and this idea will be developed throughout this chapter.

Fear of drawing

Drawing is the most easily accessible form of artistic expression, and for children it is usually a spontaneous and natural activity that is both fun and also a way of communicating their ideas, thoughts and feelings.

So why is Art and Design such a terrifying subject for teachers to teach?

Non-specialist teachers in your school may have a narrow view of what constitutes a drawing: most would agree that it involves graphic activity. You might also discover that many of them have been discouraged at a young age because they were not 'good' at drawing. In fact there is no other area of Art and Design that generates such anxiety and even resistance, and some teachers will need support to prevent them passing on their personal insecurities to children.

To develop the confidence of staff members give clear advice and guidance on how to approach drawing and how to use a range of drawing materials in the appendix of your staff Art and Design handbook or policy document.

What is drawing?

Making any mark can be read as a 'drawing'. Making a series of marks that connect to create an image which a viewer can then interpret is a 'drawing'. We know that drawing has been practised since humans first developed on our planet: handprints on cave walls are called 'drawings'. Drawing is a fundamental way for us to record, express and create.

Making an accurate copy or representation of a still life object, perhaps with a pencil, can become a dull and stressful activity for many primary school children, and yet this is often what teachers will understand as a good drawing, perhaps because this was their own experience. However there are other views, which can provide a useful tool for the primary teacher.

Many contemporary artists will refer to their work as 'drawing' when they are using a wider range of materials than a pencil. For example, one can draw in space with wire or create a drawing using string or even masking tape or textile material.

The subject coordinator could explore stereotypical perceptions of drawing by using the staff development activity at the end of this chapter.

The importance of drawing

By taking time to draw observed sources, children can develop the ability to concentrate and to think deeply. Drawing helps children to look at things properly, to 'see' them, which is an essential skill in developing an understanding of the world around them. Chapter 9: The language of Art and Design has already described how drawing can be used to explore and learn about the visual elements and visual literacy: perhaps by concentrating on line and tone, using colour, or exploring pattern and space. Remember that a teacher can develop observational activities into imaginative interpretations, or drawings may be stimulated directly from an imaginative source.

Drawing has also a key role in the design process, exploring and realising ideas in different ways, often in sketchbooks. Introducing children to a wide range of drawings by other artists will help them appreciate and learn different ways of working. In addition, pupils will simultaneously develop their visual vocabulary and their literacy skills by talking about the qualities in their drawings and the subject matter.

In your curriculum, you need to cover a full spectrum of drawing activities, recognising that pupils will draw on virtually every aspect of artistic work. Examples could include 'drawing' with a paintbrush, or making drawings through techniques such as mono-printing. Drawings can be even made with natural objects such as carefully arranged sticks or pebbles.

A survey of drawing activities in your school might reveal, perhaps to the surprise of many teachers, that they are used both incidentally and explicitly in every curriculum area.

Observational drawing

Observational work is essential in science, history and geography where it teaches children to concentrate, discover detail and to explore. Using drawing to record observations encourages children to remember what they have seen.

Teachers need to make observational drawing as interesting as possible, for example entering into a whole-class discussion about the subject first can be helpful to motivate pupils. Simple aids that will be useful include: magnifying glasses for observing in detail; cardboard tubes or rolled paper can help isolate sections of a view; L-shaped cards can be made into a viewfinder; and children could make their own special pair of binoculars using recycled materials. Encourage teachers to bring in unusual objects and always use first-hand sources.

Progression

Children should be encouraged to draw as often as possible and if they have opportunities to draw regularly from an early age they will not become self-conscious about the outcomes. As they grow older, this confidence will help them to face the challenges of secondary school.

Sketchbooks should be provided, or even handmade, and pupils encouraged to use them as visual notebooks. Drawing then becomes a creative tool, not just for carefully observed recording, but also as a form of creative visual note-taking. Pupils' progress can often be seen most clearly when looking at their sketchbooks and they are an invaluable assessment tool.

Drawing materials and processes

Avoid providing too many options at once when you are teaching drawing processes, or introducing new materials for the first time. A bewilderingly wide range of drawing materials is available and each of the materials has unique properties. As subject coordinator you can help colleagues by offering advice on which materials might be best to use for different effects. With support, pupils should be encouraged to explore each type of material.

The following items are those that no primary school Art and Design department should be without:

Chalk: white chalk can be used in combination with charcoal to highlight white or bright areas, or with coloured chalks to produce coloured drawings.

Charcoal: is an excellent cheap graphic material, ideal for working on a large scale. It favours a broader and freer approach than the pencil and is a flexible and expressive medium. Buy medium or thick sticks so that children can apply pressure without the charcoal splintering.

- Experiment with charcoal, creating dark areas by pressing hard with thick charcoal, and lighter areas by applying a softer touch.
- Encourage children to smudge the charcoal deliberately onto a white paper surface to create a range of grey tones. Use an eraser to lift out the charcoal, therefore creating a 'negative' drawing.

Compressed charcoal: invaluable for achieving very dark lines or black areas on tonal work. Charcoal-leaded pencils are also useful for fine work.

Drawing ink: available in a range of colours and is very good for teaching about 'line' and 'shape'. It can be used with a traditional pen and nib, or by dipping barbeque sticks into the ink and drawing onto prepared coloured surfaces.

Drawing paper: good quality paper, such as cartridge paper, white or coloured, textured or smooth, will bring out the best in either pencil or charcoal work. A range of other papers should also be available: from smooth to heavily textured and in different tones and colours, as this will extend the possibilities of all drawing media.

Felt-tip pen: even the humble felt-tip can produce bright colours and crisp lines. A range of colours and size of nib should be accessible for graphic work.

Graphite stick: is the inside of a pencil in a stick, and is available in the same 'B' range as pencils. These sticks are wonderful for large, free and expressive work and for creating very black or shiny areas on a drawing.

New media: see Chapter 11: Technology and new media. Drawing with digital technology is now common and David Hockney's iPad drawings are a good example of this.

Oil pastels: as the name implies, these will not mix with water but are useful because of their especially intense hue.

- Try experimenting with scratching through thick layers of oil pastel to reveal the surface underneath, and remember that they can be mixed like normal oil paints by working one colour on top of another to make different colours.
- Add some sunflower oil soaked into a cotton bud and use this to mix colours together.
- Draw a design or image with oil pastels and then wash over it with watercolour paint to achieve a resist effect.

Pencil: the ordinary pencil is actually quite a sophisticated tool. Ensure that you budget for a range of pencils (HB – 9B) and that staff understand the different degrees of softness which will provide a wide tonal range, from subtle pale greys (HB) to deep blacks (8 or 9B are the softest). Pupils should recognise the potential of pencils and learn to use them effectively.

Soft pastels: similar in texture to ordinary chalk, but produce more sophisticated and subtle colour work. The colours can be smudged together to create new tones.

Spray fixative: when using dry, soft materials, such as water-based pastels, it will be essential to 'fix' the work with a spray when it is finished to avoid smudging. This should be applied by the teacher in a well-ventilated space.

Water-based pastels: often in the form of pencils or stick pastels. They can be used as a normal colour drawing medium, but when water is added with a brush they will mix together to produce a subtle watercolour effect.

Watercolour paint: can be added to a pencil drawing using a 'wash' technique to add colour to the line drawing.

Many of the above materials can combine drawing and painting methods using different tools. As soon as it is recognised that you can draw with a stick dipped in ink, or that scraperboard or 'crayon etching' are also forms of drawing activity, it becomes a less forbidding process.

Your scheme of work should indicate when a particular medium would be appropriate for certain work, and what children should learn about its properties and potential.

Whatever is selected for drawing, it is important to provide a systematic, progressive programme if pupils are to develop their drawing confidence and expertise as they proceed through the school.

Teaching perspective

Observational drawing often involves the representation of a three-dimensional object as a two-dimensional form and this is a skill that can involve the use of perspective. However, perspective should not be taught mechanically but be introduced when required, which is usually older primary pupils who are drawing subject matter that can be most effectively represented this way. Perspective is a Western artistic convention and there are many other ways of representing space and depth in a drawing.

Staff development activity

Drawing workshop

Hold a staff meeting on drawing, making sure it is interesting, non-threatening and not judgemental. Split the staff into discussion groups and ask them to talk together for a few minutes to air any particular issues, which you can then pick up on and address throughout the session.

Prepare a wide selection of drawing materials and paper/surfaces. Explain that teachers must use only materials, or combinations of materials, that they have not tried before. They should then choose their subject from a list of activities such as:

▶ Go outside and look up at the sky. Draw what you can see.
▶ Draw an object or a person from observation using one continuous line only.
▶ Trace your journey around a room using only masking tape or string.
▶ Draw an intuitive response to these words: wobbliness; hairy; lightness; soggy; and so on.
▶ Draw an object using only a pair of scissors and a piece of sugar paper to explore 'shape' and develop hand–eye coordination.
▶ Rub charcoal across a piece of paper to make a grey surface – now use an eraser to draw into this. It will 'lift out' the charcoal and create a tonal image.

13 Painting

In primary schools there can be an assumption that all painting media have similar properties and that teachers will know how to use these. It is often given a lower priority in staff development activities than other media and processes because of this. In fact because of the vast range of paint media available, understanding their various properties is essential if they are to be used effectively. Although many pupils will paint without inhibition in the pre-school years, this free approach will not be maintained without teacher support as pupils' progress through Key Stage 2 (ages 7–11). Pupils' skills will only develop effectively if painting tools and media are introduced systematically and they are encouraged to experiment with challenging learning tasks. This chapter will explore details that the subject coordinator needs to know about what can sometimes be a neglected medium.

Paint as medium

Pupils should be given experience of a wide range of painting media, although they should not be introduced to too many at one time as this might lead to confusion. As a subject coordinator with budget restrictions you will probably want to choose one staple paint medium, such as bottled poster paint, that will be used consistently throughout the school so that pupils can gain confidence using it. This can be watered down to a thin consistency and can also be added to create textured effects.

Acrylic paint: powder paint and other basic ready-mixed colours for school use tend to have a washable binder which dries to a matt finish. Acrylic paint, although also water-based, has a binder of plastic emulsion which will dry with a permanent slight sheen. It can be expensive to purchase acrylic paint for whole-class use, but a cheaper alternative is for children to mix polyvinyl acetate (PVA) glue with powder or poster colour. This will enable very thick colours to be mixed, which can be applied to a variety of surfaces including polythene or natural materials such as stone and wood. Palette knives can provide an alternative to brushes and acrylic paint lends itself well to this method.

Oil paint: oil colours are expensive, take a long time to dry and, because they are diluted with solvents, are impractical for general use in the primary school.

If children have developed a mastery of the use of basic colour mixing with poster or powder colour, transparent watercolour and acrylic paint, and they can exploit the differing properties of each medium by the time they reach Year 6 (ages 10–11) they will be well prepared to paint with confidence in the future.

In your position as subject coordinator you should list the key learning activities for each year group in your school scheme of work in order to achieve this goal.

Powder paint: remains a popular choice for schools because, as a dry powder, pupils can mix it to discover a wide range of colours. Mixed thickly with water, or with glue, flour, sand or earth, it can be used as thick impasto and it is also useful for sprinkling onto wet paper to achieve special effects.

Ready-mix paint: the many colours on the market are user-friendly, but some are basically only powder colour mixed with water which, when their cost is considered, might make them seem an expensive convenience.

Colour mixing is a vital activity whichever type of paint is used. It can sometimes be tempting to provide children with ready-mixed secondary colours. Don't do it, because learning opportunities are missed – children should be able to see for themselves the magic of colours changing.

Watercolour paint: a better choice than powder paint as it can be mixed thinly when pupils need a transparent effect, where the white colour of the papers shows through. For very young children watercolour paint is available in large blocks, which are very effective when used with large brushes and plenty of water. Wonderful, vibrant results can be produced when painting over drawings made with candle wax or oil pastels. For very young children, solid blocks of poster colour are effective with large brushes and plenty of water. Wonderful, vibrant results can be produced when painting over drawings made with candle wax or oil pastels.

Tools and techniques

Obviously the most conventional way of applying paint is with a brush and a range of good brushes of different sizes is essential.

Different paint media require different brushes. Watercolour can be best applied using soft flexible brushes, while powder paint requires a harder bristle. Brushes come in all sizes and shapes and pupils should have the chance to choose the most appropriate brush for the task in hand.

A brush with a square end will produce a different effect from a round one; a fine brush will be needed for a delicate or detailed work and a much larger one is needed for bold, expressive mark-making.

Practice brushwork

If pupils are to learn how to use a range of brushes, it is important for them to experiment with their effects, recording the range of outcomes in their sketchbooks. Focus this experimentation by giving them words such as 'thin', 'heavy', 'hard' and 'soft' and asking them to make a range of marks to illustrate each word. Children can then challenge their classmates to match the words to the painted outcomes.

Experimental painting

The range of effects that can be produced with a brush is considerable but paint can be applied with almost anything, even pieces of card, and interesting effects can also be achieved with sponges or rags, by stippling with a stencil brush, flicking paint onto the surface using a toothbrush or even dribbling it from a stick.

Pupils will relish the opportunity to experiment with combinations of materials; for example, paint thin layers of transparent paint in a series of glazes onto tissue paper. Try mixing acrylic paint thickly with sand to create textured surfaces; scratch through one painted layer to reveal a different colour underneath; drag thick paint over a previously textured painted surface leaving some of the 'under painting' exposed. It might even be possible to design a machine that paints for you.

The aim of this experimental activity will be to develop an understanding of media properties, the potential of a variety of tools and the many methods of application. If pupils progressively increase their understanding and skills in using and controlling paint, the frustration that sets in as they become more critical of their work will be lessened.

Surfaces

Good quality cartridge or thick sugar paper is essential if the paint is to adhere satisfactorily to the surface, and the paper is to remain reasonably flat after drying. Newsprint and cheap sugar papers are unsatisfactory substitutes that should be avoided. For watercolour work, heavier, specially textured papers may be introduced, although these are expensive. Painting onto dampened paper is particularly effective if using these papers. Card or cardboard with a fairly rigid surface is needed if thick, textured paint is to be applied effectively with a palette knife.

Although acrylic paint, because of its plasticity, can be applied to almost any surface without preparation, very absorbent surfaces such as a brick wall (for a mural) may benefit from priming before the application of paint.

If non-acrylic water-based colours, including powder paint, seem disappointingly flat and dull after drying, the colour may be revitalised by being coated with a very thin PVA mixture, or even by buffing the surface to sheen with a soft cloth after spraying with furniture polish.

All pupils should have the chance of working on an easel or on paper pinned to a wall space. This will allow the children to discover how adjusting the thickness of paint can stop it from running and dripping.

Colour range

It is important to keep a wide range of colours available but not so many that it discourages the mixing of colours. Supplement a basic set of 'double primary' colours with Prussian blue, black and white. The 'double primary' system is one that has a 'hot' and 'cool' tone of each of the three primary colours (red, yellow and blue). Using this system enables children to mix a wide range of secondary and tertiary colours, as shown in the chart.

Double primary colour system

cool yellow	=	lemon
hot yellow	=	cadmium/bright yellow
cool blue	=	turquoise
hot blue	=	ultramarine/bright blue
cool red	=	crimson
hot red	=	cadmium/bright red
Prussian blue black and white		

Tip: always order twice as much yellow and white as the other colours as they get used up more quickly.

Some colours, such as an intense purple, are difficult to achieve by basic mixing and so this limited palette can include a wider range when the task demands it. For example, fluorescent colours can be useful if complementary colours are being explored through a topic such as 'carnival'.

Tints can be studied when pupils are asked to mix white, little by little, with all of the basic colours to explore pastel tones. Black can be carefully added to colours in the same way, to produce different shades. Alternatively, if black is removed from the palette pupils can be encouraged to try to mix colours in order to get a subtle range of very dark tones by adding Prussian blue.

The objective is to give pupils a broad experience when they are learning about using colour and paint. Try to encourage teachers to resist always giving children black and white or, something that can be equally inhibiting, always denying pupils black or white. At the same time, only ever allowing a very limited range of basic colours in order to ensure that outcomes are conventionally 'tasteful' should be discouraged. These will all restrict pupils' learning opportunities, when your aim is for children to gain confidence in selecting the most appropriate range of colours for the subject matter and the task in hand.

The language of colour

The most obvious visual element that will be explored by using paint is colour, although the painting process involves mark-making and the exploration of tone, line and texture as well.

The language of colour should be introduced systematically, with the scheme of work outlining the key areas of knowledge about colour that are to be acquired at each stage, including when that knowledge is to be reinforced. For instance, pupils should understand that primary colours can be mixed to produce secondary colours. They should then learn what colours can be mixed to create tertiary colours, such as browns and greys. They will develop a vocabulary of colour by seeing how many different secondary colours they can mix from two primaries, and begin to understand the difference between a tint and a shade.

An understanding of where colours sit in relation to each other on the colour wheel is important, and this can be taught without rigidly and painstakingly reproducing it.

Learning about colour should be developed through enjoying and exploring the medium of paint freely without any constrictions.

Paint workshop

As subject coordinator you should ensure that paint is used regularly, consistently and effectively across the school.

Consider staging a paint workshop for staff to experience colour mixing using the double primary system. Give them a chance to experiment freely using the full range of paint media and tools.

Make sure that all the staff are well prepared for painting. They will need mixing palettes, plenty of water for washing brushes, and a paint rag for dabbing off excess water. Keeping your brushes clean is the key to good painting. Also, something to paint on will be required.

Build in discussion time to ensure that everyone understands that the activities explore paint as a medium, and that they develop their understanding of how they might teach the visual language of colour. Pupils' confidence will grow as teacher expertise increases.

Don't take the medium of paint for granted.

14 Printmaking

Printmaking is an exciting way to explore imagary, focusing particulary on the visual elements of texture and pattern. A printed image has a unique and special quality that records surface detail very accurately in a manner that cannot be achieved in any other way. As an Art form, printmaking has many uses: not only as fine Art, but also in the world of Design, for example in textiles, fashion and architecture. Pupils can undertake scientific and environmental investigations and observations using very simple print techniques such as rubbings. Printmaking has a history that can open pupils' eyes to cultural learning as, perhaps, no other medium can.

Getting organised

It is important for you, as subject coordinator, to know that there could be a number of factors that might inhibit teachers from using printmaking with pupils. The main one is difficulty of organisation, given the large size of some primary classes, and the problems generated by a potentially 'messy' process. Ironically, printmaking usually is a very clean and inclusive activity if done well, and the results can be satisfying for all.

It is possible to introduce printmaking effectively and trouble-free as a small group activity. It is much easier to perform one demonstration to the whole class and allow each of the children to take turns after that.

Whatever the group size, it is essential to ensure that all working surfaces are covered and that pupils are wearing overalls. If working with the whole class it is preferable to have a limited number, perhaps one or two, 'inking-up stations' in the classroom. Other groups, while waiting to use the inking-up stations, can then be preparing for printing or finishing work.

Materials

Specialist equipment is necessary for printmaking and will need to be bought in. It is a good idea to keep a central resource for teachers to share so that you can keep a track of what is running low, and when you need to reorder.

You will need:

Cleaning-up materials: plenty of rags and sponges will be handy to clear up afterwards, although printmaking is ideally a very clean process.

Ink: only water-based printmaking ink should be used with primary children and there are plenty of types on the market. If the budget is tight then order black, white, red, yellow and blue as basics and these can then be mixed to create new colours.

Paper: paper can have considerable influence on the quality of a print. Thin paper that is flexible, including newsprint or coloured tissue, will often produce a better print than stiff paper with a strong texture.

Paints: it is possible to create simple prints using powder or ready-mixed paint and this can be good for work in Early Years' (below age 5) classrooms, but these materials dry too quickly to be effective for detailed block work or for mono-printing methods.

Rollers: rubber rollers of differing widths.

Trays: rigid plastic laminate sheets or plastic inking-up trays for rolling out the ink.

Processes

The most simple and effective printmaking techniques in primary schools do not require a printing press and many techniques are suitable for working with Early Years (below age 5) and Key Stage 1 (ages 5–7) pupils, but if teachers are inexperienced it is advisable to persuade them, as subject coordinator, to have a go themselves before attempting to print with a class.

Most skills in printmaking are acquired through actually doing it, although the processes need to be demonstrated first. For example, pupils will benefit from seeing how to use only the minimum amount of ink and how to roll it out evenly onto a flat surface. Commercially produced ink is ready to use straight from the tube or tin.

Found objects

A good starting point is to explore the concept that we can 'take a print from anything'. This will engage pupils in the process of visual inquiry by challenging them to print from, for example, organic forms such as leaves, differing flat wood grained planks, or any manufactured surfaces that are flat such as fabric or the soles of shoes. This is a logical extension of taking a wax crayon rubbing from a surface, such as the wall or floor, to reveal its texture and pattern. For these activities the ink or paint can be simply applied with a brush or sponge as effectively as using a roller.

It is possible to get interesting prints from the most unlikely sources. Consider, for instance, printing from an old shirt or shorts, washing-up brushes, and other household items. If you can pick it up, you can make a print from it, is a good principle. Visit the Early Years' (below age 5) classes and you will probably see a good deal of imaginative printmaking taking place as part of their daily routine. As well as printing a single impression of a found object, young pupils can combine prints from cotton reels, building blocks and any other available bits and pieces, making complicated pictures or patterns to develop compositional skills. They should also be encouraged to enrich other work such as their paintings by printing onto them with found objects, or re-using the outcomes of, for instance, a potato printing activity in a subsequent collage. Even printing from found objects is more meaningful if treated as a part of a continuous expressive project to enhance visual learning.

Block printing

Improvised printmaking processes can become more structured and complex for older pupils by building up relief printing blocks, gluing items such as string, sandpaper and other flat, textured surfaces, onto a piece of hardboard or strong card. This is known as 'relief printing' because the raised surface that is produced is inked up, and can be printed without a press by laying paper over it and rubbing vigorously. Pupils will also soon discover that it is usually best to lay the paper on top of a block and rub to make an effective print, rather than put the block onto the paper and apply pressure. Irregular shapes can also be cut out of card and glued on to the block according to a pre-planned design, which can then be used to explore repeat patterning.

Press prints

Another method of printing is to cut into a flat surface so that the sections incised do not print. The simplest and most manageable medium for this is the sheets of fine polystyrene available from Art suppliers. These are soft enough to be scored with almost anything including a pencil, or objects can be pressed into the surface to create a pattern.

The sheet is simply inked up after this procedure and the print is made. Further incisions and drawings can be added and the same block can be used to overprint with several colours. These methods can be structured into your scheme of work in varying degrees of complexity, making press printing very appealing to all ages in the primary school.

Lino may be an alternative for older pupils, but this can be an inflexible medium, even though cutting is easier if it is warmed prior to being cut into with a specialist tool. There are modern alternatives, such as 'soft-cut' block printing material, but great care must be taken as lino-cutting tools are very sharp and can easily cut pupils' hands if they slip. Children should therefore be very carefully supervised throughout the process.

Stencils

Stencil methods are another form of printmaking, and activities can vary from rolling ink across simple cut paper stencils to elementary versions of screen-printing. The latter involves squeezing ink through a silk mesh stretched over a simple frame, with a paper stencil underneath used to mask certain sections of the paper from the ink. This is best treated as a small group activity for older pupils. Art suppliers now provide a basic kit for such processes, which make them more manageable; it is essential to try this process out yourself before introducing it to pupils.

Mono printing

Of all simple primary print processes, mono printing can be the most flexible and exciting. The basic method involves painting an image on any flat, non-porous surface, such as acrylic glass or a plastic acetate sheet, and taking a print from it. Only one (mono) print can be taken. Alternatively, the complete surface can be rolled out with printing ink, with some sections subsequently removed using a finger, the end of a paintbrush or a rag before taking a print. This elementary process can be made using bought or homemade 'finger-paint' and works well with young pupils.

Multi-colour mono-prints

Another method, to be introduced as pupils' confidence and control increases, involves using a roller to spread a very thin, even film of ink onto a clean, flat surface. Thin paper is dropped lightly on to it and a drawing is made on the back of the paper. The pressure created by this means that it will pick up every fine detail of the drawing, and the paper can then be carefully moved to a different colour surface and the process repeated to produce multi-coloured linear images that are similar to an etching. You must ensure that there is only a fine film of printing ink on the surface to make a successful print.

Mixed media

Combining printmaking with other two-dimensional processes, for instance printing onto a pre-painted surface, or cutting up prints to use as collage material, or drawing or painting into an already printed image, will give more challenges. The imagery being explored should also be carefully considered, with every opportunity being taken to enhance the pupils' powers of observation, and to deepen their understanding of the visual language that they are encountering. Printmaking has much to offer if it is planned carefully, presented progressively and given similar priority to other artistic processes.

Using printmaking effectively

As subject coordinator you should encourage other staff to use printing as a part of a continuous process of visual enquiry rather than a way of only quickly producing slick and superficial end products.

Printmaking as a medium can easily be linked to many topics including those exploring other cultures, such as Japanese woodblocks.

Make sure that you have a range of examples of prints by a variety of artists for the teachers to show children as stimulus material. Start your search with: Katsushika Hokusai; Albrecht Dürer; Francisco De Goya; Rembrandt van Rijn; Pablo Picasso; Henri Matisse; Andy Warhol; Yayoi Kusama; Chuck Close; and Tracey Emin.

Suggest that all classes in your school attempt a printmaking project during one particular term and display the outcomes around the school. This will not only be an inspirational way to encourage the teachers to try something new but will also clearly show evidence of progression throughout the school.

15 | Textiles and craft

Textile work includes many craft techniques, and Art and Design education is not complete without it. Handcrafts have been declining in recent years partly because of the success of digital technology, but it is extremely important for children to develop physical skills to give them confidence in their own capabilities. Learning crafts and working with textiles will develop their resourcefulness and imagination, and can also help pupils appreciate their own and others' cultural heritage through skills handed down through generations.

Textile arts and craft

Textile artists work with fibre-based materials from natural or synthetic sources. Traditionally, these fibres would be joined by weaving, stitching, knitting, braiding, lace making and so on. Today's contemporary textile artists and crafters use a wide range of materials and techniques to make their art- or craftwork, often combining materials, such as fabrics, with non-textile materials, for example wire or paper, to produce innovative designs.

Handcraft skills are sometimes combined with new technology to produce work that is both exciting and inspirational.

Cultural education

Introducing textiles from around the world is important not only in Art and Design. Geographical and historical topics can be brought to life through activities that explore everyday life and culture, local or folk traditions, from around the world. For example they might discover which vegetables and plants can be used to extract fabric dyes in India, or look at textile techniques such as Indonesian batik, discover meanings in patterns on African kangas, or take a look at the traditional costumes of various countries.

Children can learn about different cultures through handling and making artefacts and craftwork, and you will be able to teach them about where they originate from.

Learning to craft is also a good way to provide links between school and home, and can be a positive intergenerational or community activity. You might draw on the skills of pupils' friends, relatives or local crafters to demonstrate techniques.

Life skills

It is important for primary pupils of all ages to acquire a high level of fine motor physical skills and these can be developed while making activities, which pupils enjoy and are motivated to achieve results they can be proud of. It can be quite shocking to see children at Key Stage 1 (ages 5–7) who cannot use a pair of scissors correctly, or tie a simple knot or a bow, but for some children life skills such as these can be missed entirely if they are absent at home.

Store cupboard

The best way to stock up for items that can be used for textile projects is to collect wools and yarns, fabric lengths, sacking and hessian, ribbons, plastic sheets or bags and other scrap materials that can be cut to size and used for stuffing and weaving. Many of these items can be donated, so send a quick letter to parents asking for resources and organise for some boxes or crates to be kept in a central storage area to collect them. Sort the materials into colour bands so that it is easy for teachers to see what is there.

Small off-cuts or swatches of fabric are also a useful resource. Keep these in colour band assortments in large, clear plastic wallets, so that teachers will be able to take them easily to the classrooms.

Other materials essential for textiles and crafts include the following: knitting needles, sewing and embroidery needles, and cotton and embroidery threads in a range of colours; netting, twine, beads and buttons that can be kept in clear screw-top containers; an assortment of natural materials also make excellent materials for weaving; and twigs, leaves, flowers and so on can be collected by pupils for immediate use.

You might consider joining a local scrap store where you will find many unusual recycled materials to add an imaginative element to any project. Search online for a store near to you or ask your local council if they have one. There is usually a joining fee for annual membership, but if you use the store often it will be worth every penny.

Avoid direct help

As subject coordinator, you need to explain to teachers that their role is to support and encourage pupils. When teaching crafts they should hold back from too much direct help once they have demonstrated the techniques. Children need to take ownership of their work so that they can feel the excitement and enjoyment of making something that is truly their own. The last thing you will want to see is 30 crafted artworks on display that look as though they have all been designed and made by the teacher.

Craft techniques

There are many different techniques and materials used in textile and craftwork, but here are a few particularly useful ones.

Weaving

There is no better way to teach children about textiles used for clothing and soft furnishings than by asking them to make their very own piece of fabric using a very simple, inexpensive card loom. This is a relaxing, contemplative craft with satisfying results. Pupils will discover an ancient skill and learn subject-specific vocabulary, using terms such as warp (vertical threads that hold the weaving) and weft (horizontal threads that are woven through the warp).

Cut slots (approximately 1 cm deep and the same measurement between each slit) on opposite sides of a piece of stiff card and secure one end of yarn to the outer edge. To make the warp, wrap the yarn from bottom to top by securely inserting this into each slot as you go around. Tuck the end of the yarn in at the back so that it is out of the way and you are ready to weave. To weave, start with your thread at the very bottom of the loom and weave under and over the warp, going back and forth across the card, packing the weaving down as tightly as you wish as it progresses. To release the weaving once it is finished, simply cut the warp in the middle of the back of the card and tie the fringes at either end.

Sewing

Appliqué: involves sewing pieces of fabric on top of one another, layering the material to make a design or an image. Once children have learned how to sew with a needle, cotton appliqué techniques can be used to explore class themes or topics. It can also be linked to learning about other cultures and traditional crafts. Show children examples of American quilts or the South American folk art 'Arpillera' to inspire ideas for projects.

Embroidery: use large-eyed needles, especially with young children, and coloured embroidery threads, available from educational suppliers. Cheap cotton twill, cross-stitch fabric or hessian are good fabrics for experimental embroidery as these are easy for a needle to pass through. Show pupils some simple stitches to begin with, such as running stitch, backstitch, cross-stitch and herringbone stitch.

Once children have mastered the basics they will be able to make free experimental pieces using stitches of varying sizes and adding in different yarns and twine, buttons and beads. They might create traditional cross-stitch embroidery by drawing a design onto a small piece of fabric and filling the shape with stitches.

Batik

Traditional batik is a method where a pattern or design is drawn onto fabric in melted wax with a special tool (tjanting) or paintbrush, and this is immersed into dye. The dye will not be absorbed into the fabric where the wax has been placed.

After the fabric has dried out, it is dipped in a solvent to dissolve the wax, or ironed between sheets of newspaper to absorb the wax and reveal the deep, rich colours and the fine crinkly lines that give batik its character. The process can be repeated several times to produce a final design in different colours.

Hot wax batik will require specialist equipment and although it is possible to introduce this technique to small groups of Key Stage 2 (ages 7–11) pupils, it must obviously be very closely supervised because of safety concerns.

A safer alternative can be achieved using flour paste: one cup of flour, one cup of water and four teaspoons of alum (which can be bought from a chemist shop).

These ingredients should be mixed together to form a paste and painted or squeezed from a recycled washing-up liquid bottle directly onto fabric. Dip the fabric in a dye, and allow it to dry thoroughly before carefully washing to remove the paste and reveal the design.

Knitting and knotting

These are ideal handcrafts for a willing parent or grandparent to help out with. You might consider setting up a weekly lunchtime knitting club and teach basic knitting, crochet, French knitting or macramé skills. Initially it is better to use fairly thick yarn and big needles, as these will be easier for small hands to manage, and will get rewarding results more quickly.

Creative hobbies

Very often teachers will feel more comfortable with craft and textiles techniques than other 'fine Art' activities, such as drawing and painting. This could be because many people will have creative arts as hobbies, and as the subject coordinator you can make the most of your staff's hidden talents by asking in school if any of them have a special craft or hobby to share with other members of staff.

There are many more techniques to be explored through craftwork and textile projects, such as: felt making, silk or glass painting, yarn wrapping, doll making, tie-dying, costume or head-dress making, to name but a few. It is very easy to research on the internet for step-by-step 'how to do it' instructions for these and many other techniques.

In many parts of the country, there will also be inexpensive workshops run by teachers for local colleagues. It is worth locating these – check the NSEAD website for details.

As subject coordinator it will be worth printing out a few examples of these instructions which you can laminate and add to your curriculum resources.

16 | Clay modelling

Clay is the most important and useful modelling medium in schools. Overall, three-dimensional work in the primary school could be considered an underdeveloped activity, with some pupils having little or no experience in this area. However it is an essential part of any curriculum planned by an Art and Design coordinator and modelling in clay can develop many useful skills and provide creative opportunities. Although working with clay requires some special equipment, a kiln is definitely not essential and should never prevent schools from using clay.

Modelling clay

Although Early Years' (below age 5) classrooms may well have a wider range of malleable materials, such as wet sand, mud, playdough and soap flakes, and these can all be used for pupils to explore creatively, clay is the most important resource. Three-dimensional processes can be divided into two distinct categories: 'modelling' and 'construction' (see table in Chapter 5: Planning for Art and Design). Modelling involves the manipulation of a soft, malleable medium such as clay or plaster of Paris, and 'constructing' involves building and joining with more rigid materials.

Clay can also be used for construction activities by creating coils or slabs to make three-dimensional structures and sculptures. It can even be carved into when in its 'leather hard' state. Clay is a natural material that is beautifully cool to touch and soothing to manipulate and, if your clay lesson is going well, you will notice a relaxed and easy atmosphere in the classroom.

It is a much underrated material which, with practice and regular use, can help develop pupils' fine and gross motor skills due to its weight and consistency as well as teaching children scientific concepts such as changing materials, mathematical learning including shape and measure, and language and vocabulary development through discussion and description. These features underpin the fact that clay work should be an essential and regular component in every pupil's balanced Art and Design education.

Sadly it is less used now than in the past and is sometimes regarded as a messy material and difficult to organise. However some simple procedures can make clay manageable for even very young children and it is an exciting and satisfying medium to use with every primary age.

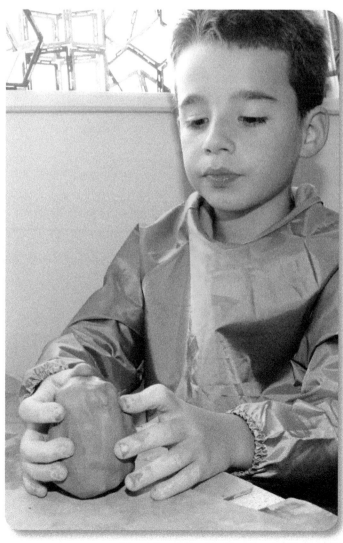

Properties of clay

Clay has traditionally been used throughout the centuries to make pots and vessels. It is, though, an exciting sculptural medium too. Interestingly, almost anything made in two dimensions can also be recreated in three dimensions with clay.

It is important that pupils develop an understanding of the properties of clay. From an early age they should be given every opportunity to enjoy and explore the medium for its own sake, they also need to know that the longer they manipulate a piece of clay the drier and more inflexible it becomes. It is important too that they know its origin – it comes from natural sources underground, and it has a special magic in changing its nature when exposed to high temperature. In this respect a link with scientific knowledge can be explicitly made.

Basic skills for clay work:
- Moulding a ball of clay by hand to form new, interesting shapes.
- Pinching a ball of clay to form a bowl or hollow shape.
- Joining pieces of clay together using liquidised clay, or slip, so that pieces do not fall off when a clay construction dries out.
- Rolling a coil with an even cross-section, using their hands.
- Using a rolling pin balanced on wooden guides to ensure consistency of thickness (rather like rolling out pastry) to produce a slab of clay that can be used for construction.
- Hollowing out a solid piece of clay in such a way as to avoid it exploding during firing.

Using clay

The same standard of work should be expected from clay activities as is demanded from drawing or painting. Pupils should be encouraged to revisit their work rather than always finish it in one session, and to add careful detail using tools and equipment appropriately. They should be taught to exploit the textural potential by pressing materials into the surface of the clay.

At times they may Design or make sketches in advance for clay projects, but working directly into the medium is just as important.

Clay can be used for observation and recording, (for example, objects such as seed pods or shoes make good subjects for observation work). It can be used imaginatively and expressively, for example on topics such as fantastic machines or magical creatures. It offers a range of possibilities for studying the work of artists, for example introducing well known sculptors and studio potters as stimulus and for research, and provides an opportunity to investigate the visual elements, such as form through free modelling, or exploring texture and patterns in surface decoration. Children will enjoy problem-solving team games with clay – challenging pupils to build the highest tower or roll the longest coil from a given amount of clay will generate intense competition. And, of course, they will enjoy making functional pots or bowls using rolled coils, or constructed from slabs. Clay's potential is enormous and the buzz of excitement when children hear that clay is to be used is a reward in itself.

Using the kiln

One of the reasons clay work is underdeveloped in schools is that teachers might feel it is essential to fire clay to produce a finished product, and a kiln may not always be available. A kiln is certainly very useful, although firing work can be a time-consuming task which will probably fall on the shoulders of the subject coordinator.

The location of a kiln is an important factor if you are considering investing in one, for current safety regulations require that it should be in a separate, lockable area that is fireproof, away from pupils and with the fumes from the kiln extracted to the open air. Even a typical small kiln suitable for a primary school that works from a 13-amp socket is a major investment and ongoing annual servicing costs will also need to be considered.

It is vital to seek professional advice before buying a kiln, and once it is installed make sure that it is well used. Another option, if you wish to fire clay work, is to ask your local secondary school, college or university if they can do this for you.

To fire...

Clay changes from its 'green' fragile dry state into the robust ceramic material we are all familiar with at a minimum temperature of about 800°C. Importantly, solid clay models should not be fired as they will not survive in the heat. Sculptures and models that you intend to fire should be hollow with a wall thickness of up to a maximum of 2 cm for a standard kiln.

The first firing (known as the biscuit firing) should be done slowly after the work has been thoroughly dried. If clay is to be glazed it needs to be fired for a second time to over 1,000°C after having been painted with or dipped into a liquid solution of the glaze. It needs to be emphasised that, as the glaze will melt during firing, the kiln needs to be packed carefully to avoid any of the objects touching each other, and there should be no glaze on the base of any of them.

Many subject coordinators decide that leaving the biscuit-ware unglazed is the most sensible solution, and the pieces can then be painted with acrylic paint if required (see Chapter 13: Painting). If you decide that glazing is an option, start simply by buying ready-mixed coloured glazes from a recognised stockist and begin experimenting. The glazes gain their bright colours in the firing stage, so results can be a little unpredictable.

...or not to fire

All is not lost if a school does not have a kiln and one is not available locally, for allowing clay sculpture to dry completely and then painting and varnishing it very carefully with a polyurethane varnish or PVA glue can produce quite a solid and reasonably permanent model.

There are, in fact, several good reasons not to fire children's clay sculptures in a kiln. First, a painted finish is a lot more controllable than with glazing.

Second, the scale of work can be much larger when it is not constrained by the size of the kiln. Third, solid models do not have to be hollowed out to avoid exploding during firing. Also, it is possible to buy clay with plastic-fibre additives which hardens without firing, although it can be difficult for small hands to use because it tends to have a very stiff consistency that makes it difficult to manipulate.

Either way, a kiln is definitely not essential and should never prevent you from using clay.

Organising clay work

Earthenware, grey or buff, or terracotta are the most common types of clays used in schools, and these are fairly cheap to buy. The clay will be delivered in thick, airtight plastic bags, which will preserve it at a workable consistency until opened. As soon as it is exposed to the air, and to the willing but warm hands of pupils, it will start to dry out. After being used by pupils any surplus clay that remains malleable can be put back into the bag with a very small amount of water added. This should then be tied up so that it is once again completely airtight and can be used another time. Ongoing work will also remain moist and workable if wrapped and sealed in plastic. Plastic dustbins are the obvious place to keep the clay when not in use, and, if space is at a premium, these can be stored in an outside shed, which might be a matter for negotiation with your caretaker.

Equipment for clay

Clay work is potentially the messiest process you are likely to use with children. Wooden, hardboard or hessian mats of about 40 cm square are an essential work surface, as clay will stick onto any non-absorbent worktop: do not attempt to allow pupils to work directly on plastic class tables for this reason. Bigger boards for large-scale work are also important.

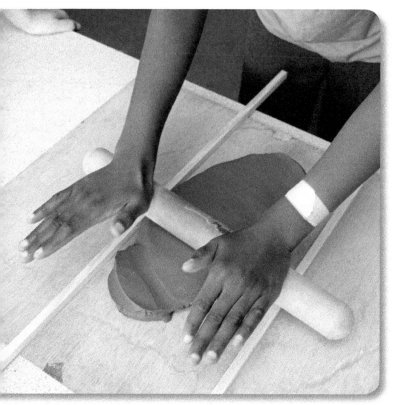

Plastic or wooden clay tools can be bought cheaply from most school equipment suppliers, although many tools for clay use can be improvised from everyday items. Blunt dinner knives and forks are helpful to make patterns; even old plastic store cards are good for slicing clay, and wire loops can easily be made to gouge holes into clay. Rolling pins and wooden guides, to ensure that the slabs that are rolled are consistent in thickness, are probably the only other tools that are needed.

Clay use in the primary school can be agreeably low on technological requirements.

Time management

It is often easier to let clay work take over the whole room for one afternoon, rather than staging a small group project continuously over several days. The advantage of this is that you can demonstrate the basic techniques and then allow pupils to experiment freely, stopping at opportune moments to encourage them to share ideas, before focusing on making a final piece. If you have a ceramic artist to work with the children, this is also the best way to maximise your visitor's time.

Children of all ages will enjoy making small-scale models but large-scale group projects will encourage team spirit and cooperation as well as creating exciting results and this will highlight the fact that clay does not always require firing. An artist such as Rebecca Warren is a good example of someone who works with clay in this way.

Tidy-up time

Dry clay dust is a health hazard, although good housekeeping will keep it to a minimum. The boards and all working surfaces, together with tools, should be cleaned at the end of every session to avoid unnecessary dust from dried clay. Any clay that is not being fired or painted should not be left exposed in the classroom. Children should of course wear aprons and these should be washed regularly; this could be a case for children wearing an adult relative's discarded shirt.

Unless there is a vital reason, it really isn't worth the effort of trying to reconstitute clay that has dried out.

Whole-class work: Chinese dragons

This work could be planned to fit in with a school Geography or PHSE focus on learning about other cultures. Ask children to research Chinese culture, including the many fantastic decorative Art forms, particularly dragons. Encourage them to share their findings on a working wall or by short group presentations. Ask them to draw their own dragon in sketchbooks or on A3-sized paper (see Chapter 12: Drawing) and pin these up as reference material during the clay project.

Begin the workshop by giving every child a piece of clay about the size of a golf ball and show them how to use one cupped hand as a mould to create a spherical form.

Having made this simple form, pupils can be encouraged to create pattern and texture on the surface using a range of different objects: squeezing clay through a garlic press, for example. The children can make as many of these forms as they wish and every completed sphere will eventually become a part of the dragon's knobbly form.

Organise the children into working groups of mixed ability. Place large medium-density fibreboard (MDF) boards onto the tables (A1-sized drawing boards are ideal).

Cover these with at least A1-sized sheets of paper and ask each group to use ideas from their sketches to draw one large simple dragon's writhing outline. Pupils can then freely use clay to create a collaborative model of a magnificent dragon, adding the spherical forms.

Pupils will learn how to make a consistent, smooth and even sphere from clay, use a range of different tools to explore surface pattern and texture, and join two pieces of clay together. They will use their imagination stimulated by their research and use problem-solving skills, negotiating and discussing with each other through working cooperatively in groups.

If you have used boards underneath the creatures, you will be able to transport the dragons to an exhibition space in the school for everyone to admire.

This project can also be successful as a whole-class activity where only one creature is made, but you would need to ensure you have cleared a good space for this.

Staff development activity

Clay workshop

Clay is a medium that even the most inhibited staff member will enjoy and use successfully with a little encouragement, so you, as subject coordinator, can raise the status of the subject in a very non-threatening and fun way. Thus, using clay is a good way to begin your staff training action plan.

Start your session by giving each teacher a ball of clay about the size of a grapefruit and no clay tools. Ask them to play with it and challenge them to find as many different ways to change the shape of the clay, making a collective list after a few minutes. They will be surprised at the many suggestions, such as curl, flatten, pinch, plait, pull, push, smash, stretch, twist and so on.

Give the teachers a blindfold and ask them to create a simple standing figure in only five minutes from their ball of clay. Many will produce a figure that is recognisable and there will be a lot of laughs as they remove the blindfolds. They will also realise that clay is first and foremost a tactile material. This is an excellent icebreaker and a good way to make staff want to work with it.

17 | Three-dimensional construction

Making a case for three-dimensional work is an important task for you as subject coordinator, because the lack of three-dimensional work in primary schools has been well documented through Ofsted reports over many years. The reasons are complex, but some staff simply do not believe that the manual skills and thought processes involved are important enough to prioritise. They are reluctant to risk the problems that might occur during the organisation and management of such physical activity in the classroom.

The importance of three-dimensional work

In Chapter 16: Clay modelling, we made the distinction between two types of three-dimensional work: modelling, which involves manipulating a flexible medium such as clay, and constructing, which is about using materials to build, such as creating sculptural forms from a wide variety of materials. To generate confidence in three-dimensional work you can encourage staff to recognise that the starting points for any sculpture or construction project can be exactly the same as for a two-dimensional activity. If a pupil can draw or paint something, be it observed or imagined, they can and should also be able to make it three-dimensional. In fact some children will respond better in this way, and boys in particular will enjoy the physical nature of three-dimensional work. It will also appeal especially to a kinaesthetic type of learner. There needs to be little or no preparatory design work, such as sketching, before making constructions, as sometimes it is quite simply more valuable to 'have a go'. You only have to watch how naturally children play with construction toys to realise how compulsive is the desire to construct.

It is important that teachers understand that the visual element of 'form' can only be explored and understood through three-dimensional activity and a broad Art and Design curriculum should always include references and introductions to the work of appropriate sculptors and sculpture.

You can also remind staff that children gain an understanding of mathematical and scientific concepts, such as weight, volume, measurement, as well as Design concepts such as problem finding and solving, through handling materials and discovering how they work.

Organisation and management

Even when staff recognise the importance of three-dimensional work, they can be put off planning this type of activity because of perceived difficulties in managing and supervising materials and processes. With class sizes in primary schools averaging 30 children it is inevitable that practical activities can pose problems, although not all three-dimensional materials are potentially messy.

Solutions will depend on the school context, but often space is a real problem, and this might have already been identified in your audit. As subject coordinator, you could suggest that teachers plan smaller-scale projects, or that three-dimensional work is a group activity, possibly managed by the classroom assistant or parent helpers. Group work is ideal for construction activities as these are naturally collaborative.

The ideal, would be a dedicated space, such as an Art room, equipped with tools, materials and workbenches, if there is the luxury of a vacant area in the school that can be claimed for this purpose.

A final possibility is to focus an annual 'Art and Design week' on a whole-school three-dimensional project, which might spread out into other open spaces in the school and playground. However, to work in three-dimensions for only one week a year does not show commitment to good practice, continuity or progression.

Problems of storage for models and sculptures can be resolved by asking pupils to record their work digitally as it progresses and before taking it home. This can also become a useful assessment exercise, as the teacher not only has a record of the process, but will also be able use the photographs to discuss ideas and thoughts and evaluate outcomes.

Simple starting points

Encourage colleagues to begin sculptural and construction techniques by collecting and using improvised materials to make sculptures from recycled materials. Cardboard boxes and containers, lolly sticks, cans, plastic bottles, discarded mechanical bits and organic objects such as fir cones can be joined together to make robots and monsters, representational models or abstract sculptures.

The very youngest of pupils can learn to use tape, glue, paperclips and elastic bands to join pieces together, and it is important to encourage progression in these skills throughout the school. Joining materials for older children might include a hand stapler to make a more permanent join, or binding together different materials using soft binding wire, or bonding card or wood with strong adhesive. Given these simple resources, pupils will improvise readily and enthusiastically and make exciting, imaginative pieces.

Problem solving

In primary schools where a creative curriculum is valued, it can be difficult to decide where Art and Design ends and Technology begins. Problem-solving activities with three-dimensional materials offer a case in point and a starting point for creative, thought-provoking work. Setting a competition to see who can build the highest tower using art straws, designing simple jewellery that moves or a hat that can be worn by two pupils, will require pupils to use materials inventively and will produce ingenious solutions without the need for significant teacher intervention.

Processes

At the same time it is important to introduce pupils to some more formal construction processes. Offer teachers a range of simple procedures that can be combined to make complex models or sculptures.

Examples might include:

- Unwanted, washed tights can be stuffed with newspaper to create snakelike creatures (look at the artist Annette Messager for some inspiration).
- Bind willow withies with tape and clad them with tissue coated with PVA glue to make large structures.
- Use brown sticky tape, foil or clingfilm to coat a three-dimensional object to make a cast.
- Roll newspaper sheets tightly into long thin spills to create structures that are surprisingly rigid.
- Use screwed-up newspaper, card or soft wire to form an armature. This can then be clad using a fabric bandage impregnated with dried powdered plaster of Paris (the material used in hospitals for supporting broken limbs). This plaster bandage can be cut into pieces with a pair of scissors, dipped and soaked in water and then wrapped around the armature. It will rapidly dry to produce a rigid sculptural form. This is a messy process that needs to be carefully supervised, but the outcomes can be impressive.

These are just some of the three-dimensional processes available for use in the primary school. However, don't fall into the trap of suggesting that three-dimensional work is difficult, messy and requires much special knowledge, as teachers could use this as a reason not to do it. Until their confidence develops, as a result of your training programme, you should encourage the use of simple materials and improvisation and experimentation should be at the centre of all practice.

Tools and safe practice

The tools needed for three-dimensional work are probably all readily available in schools and you might find them in the Design and Technology cupboard, e.g. most classrooms should have a basic set of hammers, pliers, simple saws, cutting knives, glue guns and simple safe tools which can be used for sculptural processes as well as technology activities.

Pupils should be encouraged to use these tools at a permanent workstation, with a bench and a vice if possible. Safe practice with all equipment is vital and children should be supervised closely during use and wear appropriate protective gear. As subject coordinator, should make sure that there is a current policy for using equipment safely.

In the appendix of the subject documentation, include advice on health and safety procedures. Extensive information on safe practice in Art and Design education can be found on the NSEAD website.

Without regular, progressive opportunities to work in three-dimensions, a primary pupil will not receive a broad and balanced Art and Design education. What is most likely is that the subject coordinator will have to convince hard-pressed, non-specialist staff that this is an essential part of pupils' creative Art and Design experience. The best way forward is to demonstrate by example, and you can make an impact by displaying three-dimensional work, that you have made with children, in the school's communal public spaces (see Chapter 7: Developing a creative climate). For example, it is possible to build an elaborate jungle in a corridor or entrance hall, with trees made from cardboard tubes, branches from twisted paper and multi-coloured leaves and fronds made by the children, or you could even build a snow sculpture in the school grounds, weather permitting. The enthusiasm with which pupils engage in such activities, the sense of wonder generated when others view the results and the overall impact on the environment will encourage teachers to introduce three-dimensional work to their pupils.

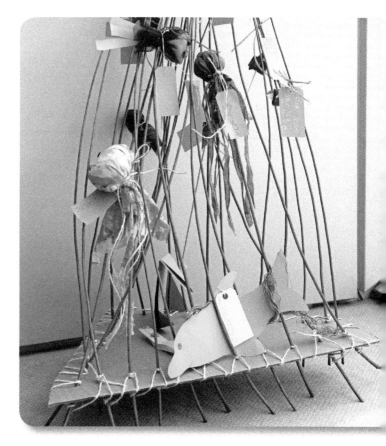

18 Design and designing

Design involves producing something that 'works' and is at the same time visually satisfying. As subject coordinator, you can give Design status in the curriculum, and help teachers make pupils aware of its relevance to every part of daily life. Design is important to a country's economic success: in fact, the UK has an enviable reputation for creativity and innovation which will continue to flourish if children have the right skills. However, if primary teachers lack confidence teaching design they may rely on templates, or avoid the subject altogether.

What is Design and designing?

What does the word 'Design' mean? One definition could be: 'to work something out by making a sketch or plan'. Often 'Design' is seen in terms of improvement of an initial idea, increasing its beauty and usefulness. The former chairman of the Design Council, George Cox, wrote: 'Design is what links creativity and innovation. It shapes ideas to become practical and attractive propositions for users or customers. Design may be described as creativity deployed to a specific end' (*The Cox Review,* 2005).

Design in the classroom

Encourage teachers to get children to look for examples of Design. Their list will soon include everyday items from lunch boxes to pencils.

It might be a good challenge for them to find something that has not been through a Design process as this will reinforce the concept that without Design there would be no 'stuff'.

The built environment

Perhaps the easiest way to begin is with a walk around the school. Ask children to consider the look, feel and use of the school building: why are the bricks a certain colour or shape? Or why do some of the windows seem to allow more light in than others? Consider the relative heights of ceilings, the floor coverings chosen, and observe the relationships between colours that have been selected for particular areas. Do you have any architectural plans available to show the children?

A simple activity could be to document the way the school looks through photographing areas and then matching these to the architectural plan.

Looking and observing

Children can consider Design features in their own classroom. For example, ask them to look at the interactive whiteboard. Why is it in that position? What about doors and windows? What sort of decisions would have been made in designing the room? What would an ideal classroom look like? Ask the children to make a list of items that you all agree should be included, and let them work out new designs of their own in groups.

Share the designs and evaluate them. There may even be an idea you can use in your next classroom change-around. In this way, children can begin to understand the many factors that architects and interior designers have to consider.

Cross-curricular links

Consider making a simple animated film involving a link with Literacy as children write storyboards and design titles, and with History if you use old photographs to compare 'then and now'. For example, a school visit might give you the opportunity to show how grand Victorian railway stations have design features rooted in the practical demands of technology of their time. The high, arching roofs create a wonderful sense of space today, but they were originally designed this way to allow people to move around underneath the steam and smoke that came from the trains, which rose upwards. This is captured in many paintings from that era.

Application in teaching

The important thing is to show children practical applications of Design. There are many ways to do this from looking at a local supermarket to designing a school logo. You could also encourage older children to Design a newsletter or magazine, or even ask a local website designer to visit.

Creative approaches

As subject coordinator you will want to ensure that Design is revisited in your scheme of work throughout a child's primary school education. In the Early Years (below age 5), children should have a free choice 'making area' where they can join a wide variety of materials with tape, string and glue. As they move through Key Stages 1 and 2 (ages 5–11), they should be challenged to use more sophisticated ideas and materials, including recycled materials. They should learn to use sketchbooks and digital photography to record and experiment and, even if their ideas do not work, persist at a task by re-evaluating and having another go. It is all part of the creative process. ICT could speed up some of these experiments, as they can consider alternative layouts, and so on using computer software. Having considered their designs, the children can go on to use different media, skills and knowledge from all areas of the Art curriculum to create and fulfil their Design projects.

Staff development activity

Focus on Design

Use a staff meeting or Inset day to:

▶ Ask all the staff to take a walk around the school environment, focusing on the Design of things both inside and outside. Ask them informally what Design experiences they have already had.

▶ Make a list of any local designers and craftspeople who might be willing to come into school to discuss their work with the children. Also include possible interesting places, galleries and museums to visit.

▶ Try out some ideas together before using them in class.

▶ Gather together a random selection of objects and a range of Design materials. Ask teachers to choose one of the objects and Design a bag specifically to hold it. The bag Design should reflect what it holds in both size and strength, as well as the amount of protection required to keep the object safe.
This can be great fun as well as showing how to develop imaginative and individual responses to a Design brief.

Appendix 1: Subject coordinator's checklist

Answer yes or no to these questions.

1. Preparing for subject leadership

a. Does the subject coordinator have an Art-trained background at least equivalent to GCSE Advanced level, or Art-specialist teaching education?   Yes / No

b. Does the subject coordinator have the knowledge and confidence to monitor regularly through lesson observation the delivery of the subject in classrooms throughout the school?   Yes / No

c. Does the subject coordinator have only Art and Design within their management brief in the school?   Yes / No

d. Has the subject coordinator attended any Art and Design continuing professional development (CPD) courses recently?   Yes / No

e. Will the subject coordinator be allocated some specific non-contact time for development activity in the subject?   Yes / No

f. Has the subject coordinator made contact with NSEAD or any regional network of colleagues?   Yes / No

2. Management of the subject

a. Has Art and Design been identified as a development area in your school in the last five years?   Yes / No

b. Does your school have a written Art and Design policy which reflects the current situation?   Yes / No

c. If yes, does this policy cover all of the key areas identified (in Chapter 2: What is an Art and Design coordinator?) on policy content?   Yes / No

d. Does your school have an overall plan/scheme of work for the subject that identifies skills, knowledge and understanding that is progressively developed across the key stages?   Yes / No

e. Do all members of staff follow the scheme of work?   Yes / No.
How do you know?

_____

_____

_____

_____

_____

f. Has the subject coordinator addressed other staff about key issues in Art and Design for the purpose of development at either a staff meeting or on a training day (i.e. in the last three years)?   Yes / No

g. Has time been allocated for lesson observation, scrutiny of pupils' work, learning walks, lesson plan/ evaluation and so on?   Yes / No

h. Is there a development plan for Art, which has responded to the findings of the last inspection report? (This could be either for your particular school or a subject survey inspection.)   Yes / No

3. Curriculum provision and balance

a. Does your school already ensure that artists, designers and craftspeople of both genders and a range of cultures are introduced systematically into the school?   Yes / No

b. In your school, do all pupils in each year group, every year:

    i. Engage in observation-recording and recall activities?   Yes / No

    ii. Work from imaginative/fantasy sources?   Yes / No

    iii. Explore the visual elements on a systematic basis?   Yes / No

    iv. Learn new processes and explore new media?   Yes / No

    v. Draw, paint, stick, print, model and construct?   Yes / No

    vi. Engage in practical activities with works of Art that are not based solely on copying them?   Yes / No

    vii. Work in three dimensions for at least 25% of their allocated Art time?   Yes / No

    viii. Discuss and learn about key artists, craftpeople, designers and Art from different periods and cultures?   Yes / No

    ix. Work at a variety of scales and levels?   Yes / No

    x. Keep a personal sketchbook?   Yes / No

4. Teaching style

a. Across the whole of your school, are pupils given opportunities to finish their work after a period of time, as well as completing work in one lesson?   Yes / No

b. In all classes, are pupils taught Art and Design as a specific focused subject, as well as engaging in Art arising from topic or cross-curricular activities?   Yes / No

c. Are all pupils given some direct instruction in the subject, and allowed to experiment?   Yes / No

d. Are pupils encouraged to explore media freely?   Yes / No

e. Do pupils work on Art and Design:

    i. individually?   Yes / No

    ii. in a group?   Yes / No

    iii. as a whole class?   Yes / No

5. Provision and resources

a. Is money allocated each year per child for consumable resources?   Yes / No

b. In addition, is money allocated each year per child for development work?   Yes / No

c. Does your school have adequate consumable resources to undertake all of the processes listed in section 3 above?   Yes / No

d. Are there tools for three-dimensional work available in each classroom, or that are accessible on request?   Yes / No

e. Is there a sink and a suitable 'wet area' in each room/area?   Yes / No

f. Is there adequate space in each room for work at a variety of scales and in different media?   Yes / No

g. Is there a set of reproductions of artworks at an adequate scale for whole-class discussion that can be circulated around classes?   Yes / No

h. Are there digital cameras available for Art and Design in your school?   Yes / No

i. Is there computer access whenever required and is appropriate software available for manipulating digital imagery?   Yes / No

6. Allocation of time

a. Is at least one hour a week allocated across your school specifically for Art and Design activities?   Yes / No

b. Has additional 'enrichment' time been specifically allocated for the subject – such as an Art week or an artist who visits the school?   Yes / No

c. Is there an after-school or lunchtime Art and Design club?   Yes / No

d. How are gifted and talented pupils supported in Art and Design?

_____

_____

_____

_____

_____

_____

_____

7. Assessment procedures

a. Does your school:

   i. use an assessment portfolio, with a range of children's work available?   Yes / No

   ii. have a set of agreed standards available to help staff in making judgements and moderating children's work?   Yes / No

   iii. make sure that members of staff, receiving pupils from a previous year-group/teacher, have a clear idea of each pupil's ability in Art and Design?   Yes / No

   iv. record and transfer pupils' work from one class to another as they progress through the school?   Yes / No

b. Are certain activities repeated as the pupil goes through the school to identify progress?   Yes / No

c. Do pupils evaluate their personal work and that of other pupils on a regular basis?   Yes / No

d. Do pupils record or share their work with the community? (For example, by staging exhibitions or website galleries.)   Yes / No

8. Finally

a. Were there questions you could not answer, or that raised issues you would like to later incorporate in your action plan?   Yes / No

If yes, please tell us what they are.

_____

_____

_____

_____

_____

_____

_____

_____

_____

_____

_____

_____

_____

_____

_____

Appendix 2:
Subject coordinator's staff questionnaire

Dear

I would be very grateful if you could complete this questionnaire which will be used to create a training programme and prioritise areas for whole-school development in Art and Design. Please be as honest as possible and do not be afraid to state any limitations or concerns.

Please return to me by __ / _____ / ____ .

Thank you.

1. How important do you think that Art and Design is within the primary curriculum?

    Unimportant   1   2   3   4   5   Important

    Please give your reasons:

    _____

    _____

2. Please rate your confidence to teach the following processes of Art and Design.
   1 indicates very unconfident and 5 represents very confident.

Drawing	1	2	3	4	5
Painting	1	2	3	4	5
Printmaking	1	2	3	4	5
Clay work	1	2	3	4	5
Three-dimensional work/sculpture	1	2	3	4	5
New media/photography	1	2	3	4	5
Crafts	1	2	3	4	5
Using artists' work/history of Art and Design	1	2	3	4	5
Visual elements of Art and Design	1	2	3	4	5

3. Is there any other aspect of the subject you would like support in teaching?

   _____

   _____

4. Which of the following do you do regularly with your pupils? Please tick all that apply:

   Drawing; painting; printing; three-dimensional modelling; three-dimensional constructing ☐

   Designing and pattern-making ☐

   Critical studies ☐

   Traditional crafts; photography/film; looking at or using artists' work ☐

   Other art activities not included above (please specify) ☐

   _____

   _____

5. When you teach Art and Design do you:

    a. Identify learning intentions and discuss these with pupils before you start?
      Usually / Sometimes / Rarely

    b. Show children the potential uses of materials and demonstrate techniques?
      Usually / Sometimes / Rarely

    c. Intervene if you see that pupils are having problems with an activity?
      Usually / Sometimes / Rarely

    d. Address the class collectively as well as individually during the lesson?
      Usually / Sometimes / Rarely

    e. Create time at the end of the lesson to reflect on what has happened and celebrate success?
      Usually / Sometimes / Rarely

6. Who is involved in teaching Art and Design in your class? Please tick all that apply:

You / Teacher ☐

Teaching Assistant / Learning Support Assistant ☐

Parent ☐

Other (please specify) ☐

_____

7. Who plans the Art and Design in your class? Please tick all that apply:

You / Teacher ☐

Teaching Assistant / Learning Support Assistant ☐

Parent ☐

Other (please specify) ☐

8. How much time do you devote to teaching Art and Design as a separate subject each term?

_____

9.   **a.** How much Art and Design activity arises from other areas of the curriculum?

    _____

    b. Do you consider that Art and Design subject matter is covered adequately by Art and Design-based cross-curricular work?

    Usually / Sometimes / Rarely

10. Do you feel confident in assessing children's work in Art and Design?

Yes / Usually / Sometimes / No (please give more detail here if possible)

_____

_____

11. Do any of the following restrict your teaching of this subject? Please tick all that apply:

Lack of personal expertise or knowledge ☐   Lack of space ☐

Lack of available materials/resources ☐   Demands of Literacy and Numeracy ☐

Lack of equipment ☐   Other challenges (please specify) ☐

_____   _____

12. Do you find the school policy for Art and Design helpful?

Yes / No   If no, how could it be changed to make it a more useful document?

_____

_____

13. Are there any changes that could be instituted within the school as a whole that would help you to teach Art and Design more effectively?

Yes / No   If yes, please describe these briefly:

_____

_____

14. Having thought about your practice in Art and Design, would targeted in-service training be helpful, and would you be willing to attend?

Yes / No   If yes, please identify the area/activity you would want such training to concentrate upon:

_____

_____

15. Which of the following would be useful to help you develop in this subject area? Please rate 1 (poor)–3 (good).

a. Observing an outstanding teacher teaching Art and Design. ☐

b. A team-teaching lesson in which you worked together with the Art and Design coordinator. ☐

c. The Art and Design coordinator observing your lesson and offering a view on your performance afterwards. ☐

16. Are there any other comments that have not been identified in this questionnaire?

_____

_____

_____

_____

_____

_____

_____

_____

Thank you for completing this questionnaire.

Index

Further reading and resources

There are now some excellent sources of information available for teachers. Those listed here are only a sample that you may wish to explore further.

Books

Key, P. and Stillman, J. (2009) *Teaching Primary Art and Design*. Exeter: Learning Matters.

Meager, N. (2012) *Teaching Art: Ages 4–7*. London: Belair.

Meager, N. (2012) *Teaching Art: Ages 7–11*. London: Belair.

Watts, R., Cox, S., McAuliffe, D. and Grahame, J. (2007) *Teaching Art and Design 3–11*. London: Continuum.

Wenham, M. (2003) *Understanding Art: A Guide for Teachers*. London: Paul Chapman.

Magazines

AD Magazine – published by NSEAD.

StART magazine – previously published by NSEAD: archived copies available to members at: www.nsead.org

Websites

Axis – an online database of contemporary artists: www.axisweb.org/

Baltic Contemporary Gallery, Gateshead – primary resources: www.balticmill.com/

Courtauld Institute, London (including online resources): www.courtauld.ac.uk/

Cultural Learning Alliance – a collective voice working to ensure that all children and young people in the UK have meaningful access to cultural experiences: www.culturallearningalliance.org.uk/

Engage – a membership organisation representing gallery, Art and education professionals in the UK and in 15 countries worldwide: www.engage.org/

Eridge Trust – grants for educational trips and projects in museums and galleries: www.nsead.org/

Mr Jennings – useful self-assessment in Art and Design sheets developed for primary schools. The critera suggested here can also be used to guide teacher/pupil conversations in an informal way: http://mrjennings.co.uk/

National Gallery – Take One Picture project: www.takeonepicture.org.uk/

NSEAD – information on Art education, advocacy and Regional Network Groups: www.nsead.org/

Royal Academy, London – with examples of archived resources for teachers published for each exhibition: www.royalacademy.org.uk/

Skills in the Making – includes useful information sheets on using materials: www.themaking.org.uk/

Tate Galleries, London, Liverpool and St Ives – includes online resources published for teachers: www.tate.org.uk/

Tate Tools – free downloadable PowerPoint resources: www2.tate.org.uk/tatetools/

Turner Contemporary Gallery, Margate, Kent – includes resources published for teachers: www.turnercontemporary.org/learn/resources